Hayefield Favo

Tried and True
Perennials

Copyright © 2012 Nancy J. Ondra
Second edition December 2012

Text, photography, design, and layout by Nancy J. Ondra

All rights reserved. No part of this publication may be reproduced or distributed in any form or by any means without the prior permission of the author.

ISBN-13: 978-1463510589
ISBN-10: 1463510586

Printed in the United States of America by CreateSpace

If you receive a defective copy of this book, please contact the seller for a replacement.

Title page: Purple coneflower (*Echinacea purpurea*) with golden lace (*Patrinia scabiosifolia*), spike gayfeather (*Liatris spicata*), 'The Blues' little bluestem (*Schizachyrium scoparium*), orange coneflower (*Rudbeckia fulgida* var. *fulgida*), 'Karl Foerster' feather reed grass (*Calamagrostis* x *acutiflora*), and Joe-Pye weed (*Eutrochium maculatum*) [late July]

Right: Ironweed (*Vernonia*) seedheads [mid-October]

Contents

Amsonia (bluestars) 8
Baptisia (false indigos) 14
Calamagrostis (feather reed grasses) 20
Echinacea (purple coneflowers) 24
Eutrochium (Joe-Pye weeds) 30
Helianthus (sunflowers) 36
Heuchera (heucheras) 40
Molinia (moor grasses) 44
Panicum (switch grasses) 48
Patrinia (patrinias) 54
Pennisetum (fountain grasses) 58
Persicaria (fleeceflowers) 62
Rudbeckia (orange coneflowers) 68
Sanguisorba (burnets) 72
Stachys (lamb's ears) 76
Stipa (pony tail grasses) 80
Symphyotrichum (asters) 84
Symphytum (comfreys) 90
Vernonia (ironweeds) 94
Veronicastrum (Culver's roots) 98
Index 103

'Cassian' fountain grass (*Pennisetum alopecuroides*) with aromatic aster (*Symphyotrichum oblongifolium*) [mid-October]

Introduction

If there's one thing I've learned in years of blogging, it's that "favorite plants" never fails as a great conversation starter among gardeners of all regions and experience levels. It's fascinating to find out how the favorites we share with other gardeners perform in different climates and growing conditions. Getting inspired by the enthusiasm of other gardeners for their own favorites is also an exciting way to learn about plants that we haven't yet tried.

I never get tired of writing about my own favorite plants, except for the frustration of trying to narrow them down into one list, because my choices change from season to season and year to year. The 20 I've featured here aren't the most intriguing rarities or the trendiest new introductions: they're the hardy perennials I turn to time after time because they're dependable performers in my southeastern Pennsylvania garden. Your mileage, as the saying goes, may vary. But I hope you enjoy exploring some of the species and selections that have shown themselves to be perennial stars in the plantings here at Hayefield.

Nan
www.hayefield.com

Tatarian aster (*Aster tataricus*) with golden lace (*Patrinia scabiosifolia*) [mid-October]

Now, the Plants...

Amsonia

Bluestars

**Apocynaceae
Dogbane Family**

Sturdy and dependable Arkansas bluestar (*Amsonia hubrichtii*) is one of my most favorite perennials for filling lots of space at the front to middle of a border.

- Full sun to partial shade
- Adapts to a range of soil conditions
- 2-3 feet tall; 3-4 feet wide
- Zones 4-9

✓ Seldom needs division
✓ Pests are rarely a problem
✓ Fall color is fantastic

× Takes a few years to fill out
× Can self-sow prolifically

Arkansas bluestar begins the season as a distinctly vertical to slightly vase-shaped clump. It blooms through most of May here, with clusters of starry, light blue flowers.

As the flowers finish, the stems begin to branch out just below the fading flower clusters. The weight of the bushy stem tips and developing seedheads gradually pulls the stems outward, so the plants become much wider as the season progresses.

I like to let a few young plants set seed each year but cut established clumps back hard (down to 4 to 6 inches) in late May or early June. That removes the seedheads before they ripen and encourages dense regrowth from the base, so the clumps don't flop open later in the season.

Arkansas bluestar with 'Frau Dagmar Hastrup' rose and 'Angelina' sedum (*Sedum rupestre*) [late May]

Better Together

Arkansas bluestar's powder blue blooms look particularly good with other blues, pinks, yellows, and whites. In summer, the rich green of its needle-thin but feather-soft leaves is especially pretty paired with whites, silvers, and grays, and contrasted with big, broad leaves.

Arkansas bluestar is an ideal bedmate for small spring bulbs, and for covering the bases of taller summer bulbs, such as lilies and ornamental onions (*Allium*). Just be careful when you cut back the bluestar after bloom, so you don't cut the bulb stems too.

Top left: Arkansas bluestar with 'Purple Smoke' false indigo (*Baptisia*) [mid-May]

Top right: Arkansas bluestar with giant fleeceflower (*Persicaria polymorpha*) [late May]

Left: Arkansas bluestar with 'Karl Foerster' feather reed grass (*Calamagrostis* x *acutiflora*), 'Silver Fern' ghost bramble (*Rubus thibetanus*), and the buds of drumstick chives (*Allium sphaerocephalon*) [early July]

On the Edge

Post-and-rail fencing fits well with the rural setting here at Hayefield, and I like the way it creates a sense of enclosure without blocking the view. As with any kind of fence, though, it creates a maintenance issue, in the form of trimming or weeding around the posts.

Planting Arkansas bluestar next to or even directly under the rails has been a good solution: it's dense enough to smother many weeds but billowy enough to create a gentle transition between the garden and the grass or gravel on the other side.

Planting shrubs directly against a fence could provide some of the same benefits, but then it's hard to reach the fence when it needs to be repaired or re-stained. With the bluestar underplanting, the fence is easily accessible from late fall through early spring, when the plants are dormant.

Top: Arkansas bluestar in late May
Middle: Mid-September
Bottom: Late October

10

Autumn Glory

Spectacular fall color is the feature I like best about Arkansas bluestar. It's usually a clear to golden yellow, often with some orangey tints. Full-sun clumps can also take on a reddish blush. The foliage color starts to develop in late September and continues through much of October. It can be showy even into November if the weather is mild.

Top left: Arkansas bluestar with 'Dimity' dwarf fleeceflower (*Persicaria affine*); the red foliage of Japanese blood grass (*Imperata cylindrica* 'Rubra') and a Japanese maple (*Acer palmatum*); the broad blue-green leaves of couve tronchuda (*Brassica oleracea* var. *costata*); and the tiny flowers of 'Lady in Red' Texas sage (*Salvia coccinea*) [late October]

Top right: Arkansas bluestar with the flowers of pink muhly grass (*Muhlenbergia capillaris*) [mid-October]

Left: Arkansas bluestar with the dead stems of 'Carin' Joe-Pye weed (*Eutrochium maculatum*) and feathery dog fennel (*Eupatorium capillifolium*) [late October]

Into the Winter

Once there's a hard freeze, the foliage of Arkansas bluestar finally droops and turns from yellow to tan, but it may hang on for many weeks after that. The fine-textured mounds continue to add garden interest well into winter, especially when outlined with heavy frost, encased in ice, or dusted with light snow.

The thin stems are surprisingly resilient and can persist until they're flattened by a heavy blanket of wet snow or until you cut them down in late winter or early spring, before or just as the new growth appears.

Top: Arkansas bluestar with 'Angelina' sedum (*Sedum rupestre*) [late December]

Right: Arkansas bluestar with 'Carin' Joe-Pye weed (*Eutrochium maculatum*) [late November]

Other Bluestars

Arkansas bluestar (*Amsonia hubrichtii*) is the species I've used most widely here at Hayefield, but I do have a few others around.

'Blue Ice' is a selection of uncertain origin, but reportedly with Eastern bluestar (*A. tabernaemontana*) as at least one of the parents. It's not nearly as interesting as Arkansas bluestar, in my opinion: ordinary in bloom (there are plenty of other short blue flowers for spring), nondescript in leaf, and with yellowish green fall color. Ho hum.

Hybrids between eastern bluestar and Arkansas bluestar, on the other hand, can be just as good as the latter parent. They frequently appear where both species are planted near each other. They're somewhat variable in size and vigor, with slender but not needle-thin leaves. Their flowering and growth habit are like those of Arkansas bluestar, and they share the fabulous fall color, too.

Top: 'Blue Ice' hybrid bluestar [late May]

Above: Hybrid bluestar with hydrangea, Joe-Pye weed (*Eutrochium maculatum*), silver willow (*Salix alba* var. *sericea*), giant fleeceflower (*Persicaria polymorpha*), and variegated moor grass (*Molinia caerulea* 'Variegata') [late July]

Baptisia

False or Wild Indigos

Fabaceae
Pea Family

False indigos (*Baptisia*) don't fit my usual criteria for must-have perennials, but their spring show has earned them a place here.

- Full sun to light shade
- Average, well-drained soil
- 3-5 feet tall; 3-6 feet wide
- Zones 4 or 5-9

✓ Tough and trouble-free
✓ Stunning in bloom

× Take up a lot of space
× Mostly a single season of interest

'Screamin' Yellow', a selection of *Baptisia sphaerocarpa*, gets all the credit for turning me on to using false indigos in the garden. This species is native to the south-central United States, but it's reportedly hardy into Zone 5, at least, and certainly hardy here in Zone 6.

I've never grown the straight species, but this cultivar is said to be even more compact and free-flowering. It's a show-stopper during its month-long (June) bloom period, with well over a hundred spikes on a single clump. The plants reach just 2 to 3 feet tall in flower, but the tops spread out to fill an area 4 to 5 feet across.

'Screamin' Yellow' false indigo with 'Cramer's Plum' love-in-a-mist (*Nigella damascena*), 'Caradonna' salvia, eglantine or sweet briar rose (*Rosa rubiginosa*), giant fleeceflower (*Persicaria polymorpha*), silver willow (*Salix alba* var. *sericea*), hydrangea, and pony tail grass (*Stipa tenuissima*) [early June]

14

Perennial Partners

The false indigos typically flower from mid-May to early or mid-June here in southeastern Pennsylvania — peak bloom time for many other perennials as well, including bearded irises, bluestars (*Amsonia*), catmints (*Nepeta*), hardy geraniums, and perennial salvias. They look splendid with roses and weigelas, too.

Above: 'Screamin' Yellow' false indigo with 'Walker's Low' catmint (*Nepeta*) and 'Caradonna' salvia [late May]

Left: 'Screamin' Yellow' false indigo with 'Susanna Mitchell' marguerite (*Anthemis*) [early June]

Beyond Bloom

As a group, false indigos aren't very exciting after bloom, but they're good for filling space. 'Screamin' Yellow' has a particularly neat, mounded habit, especially the first few years. Older plants can be loose and sprawling, so I often cut them back by about half as soon as the blooms fade to get more-compact regrowth.

The down side of shearing 'Screamin' Yellow' is that it removes the seedpods, which are brown and oblong instead of gray-black and elongated, as on other false indigos. Both the seedpods and the frost-killed stems stick around for months, creating an attractive presence in the winter garden.

Top left: 'Screamin' Yellow' false indigo left unsheared [late June]

Top right: 'Screamin' Yellow' false indigo winter presence [early December]

Right: 'Screamin' Yellow' false indigo seedpods [mid-December]

A Mellower Yellow

'Screamin' Yellow' has performed so well for me that I decided to try out some of the other baptisia species and hybrids. 'Carolina Moonlight', a hybrid between *B. sphaerocarpa* and the white *B. alba,* has light yellow flowers that combine prettily with rosy pinks, blues, and purples.

The bushy plants reach 3 to 4 feet tall and wide, creating shrub-sized clumps. 'Carolina Moonlight' isn't as showy as 'Screamin' Yellow' in bloom, but it's as trouble-free as other false indigos, so it's nice for May-to-June color in low-maintenance areas.

Top: 'Carolina Moonlight' and 'Purple Smoke' false indigo with Arkansas bluestar (*Amsonia hubrichtii*) [mid-May]

Left: The dusky purple-black stems and buds of 'Carolina Moonlight' [mid-May]

Exploring More Hybrids

Yellows aren't the only color options for false indigos. 'Purple Smoke', a cross between blue *B. australis* and white *B. alba*, is a vigorous grower reaching about 4 feet tall and 4 to 5 feet across, with light purple flowers.

And then there's Twilite Prairieblues ('Twilite'), a hybrid of blue *B. australis* and yellow *B. sphaerocarpa*. It's an odd grayish purple with touches of yellow and orange.

Both 'Purple Smoke and Twilite Prairieblues are pretty up close, but they don't make much of a show from a distance.

Top: Twilite Prairieblues false indigo against 'Red Majestic' contorted hazel (*Corylus avellana*) [late May]

Right: 'Purple Smoke' false indigo with Arkansas bluestar (*Amsonia hubrichtii*) [mid-May]

18

Basic Baptisias

Years ago, our options for false indigos were much more limited. The most readily available one was the species *Baptisia australis,* known as blue false indigo, and it's still worth growing. Its rich blue flowers look terrific against yellow or dark foliage, or with white flowers.

Some people rave about the gray-black seedpods, but I don't find them attractive, and I remove them when I shear the plants back by half after bloom.

White false indigo (*B. alba*) is also eye-catching in bloom, and the dark stems and buds are very elegant. This species has a much more open habit than the others. So far, I haven't included it in the garden, because I think it's at its best mingling with grasses in the meadow.

Both of these species are hardy in Zones 4 to 9, at least.

Top: Blue false indigo (*Baptisia australis*) [mid-May]

Above: Blue false indigo with giant fleeceflower (*Persicaria polymorpha*) [late May]

Right: White false indigo (*B. alba*) in meadow [early June]

Calamagrostis

Feather Reed Grasses

Poaceae
Grass Family

'Karl Foerster' feather reed grass (*Calamagrostis* x *acutiflora*) is one ornamental grass that I wouldn't want to garden without.

- Full sun to partial shade
- Average, well-drained to moist soil
- 5 feet tall; 12-18 inches wide
- Zones 4-9

✓ Outstanding for verticality
✓ Nearly year-round interest
✓ Doesn't self sow

✗ No fall color

When I need a plant to add height but not take up much horizontal space, I turn to 'Karl Foerster'. Single clumps can be useful for adding vertical accents to beds and borders, but I like them even better in multiples.

Set out in a straight line, they're perfect for creating a screen or softening the line of a fence or wall. Within borders, it's easy to weave groupings of three or more among other perennials to create a naturalistic effect.

Wherever it grows, 'Karl Foerster' is invaluable for adding movement to the garden, because its tall, slender stems and feathery plumes wave in the slightest breeze.

'Karl Foerster' feather reed grass with 'Blaze' little bluestem (*Schizachyrium scoparium*), pink muhly grass (*Muhlenbergia capillaris*), 'Big Ears' lamb's ears (*Stachys byzantina*), and Joe-Pye weed (*Eutrochium maculatum*) [mid-August]

Spring and Summer Splendor

'Karl Foerster' feather reed grass is a cool-season grass, producing new growth as soon as the weather begins to warm in March. The rich green clumps thicken through spring, then send up their flowering stalks in late May to early June.

The plumes are pinkish, loose, and feathery at first, aging to brown with a somewhat spikier form. Rain can cause the plume-laden stems to bend dramatically, but don't try to knock off the water or you may damage the stems; leave them alone and they'll straighten up on their own as they dry.

Top left: 'Karl Foerster' with 'Lemon Lace' silver lace vine (*Fallopia baldschuanica*) [early June]

Top right: 'Karl Foerster' with 'Sutherland Gold' elderberry (*Sambucus racemosa*) [early July]

Left: 'Karl Foerster' with purple coneflower (*Echinacea purpurea*) [mid-July]

The Show Goes On

Some cool-season grasses look pretty scrappy after they bloom — at least until the weather cools off again — but not 'Karl Foerster' feather reed grass. The flowering stalks bleach to a light tan color by fall but hold their structure well, and the foliage stays green through the growing season. The plants continue to have a presence through the winter, until cut to the ground in March, around the time new growth appears.

One of the best things about 'Karl Foerster' is that it does not set seed, so you never have to cut the plants down early to avoid dealing with unwanted seedlings.

Top: 'Karl Foerster' feather reed grass with 'Big Ears' lambs ears (*Stachys byzantina*), 'Blaze' little bluestem (*Schizachyrium scoparium*), and pink muhly grass (*Muhlenbergia capillaris*) [late October]

Right: 'Karl Foerster' with pink muhly grass, coneflowers (*Echinacea* and *Rudbeckia*), and other seedheads [mid-December]

Another Calamagrostis

Korean feather reed grass (*Calamagrostis brachytricha*) is much harder to find than 'Karl Foerster', but it's worth hunting for. You'd hardly guess they were related, because the two grasses have rather different habits. The foliage of Korean feather reed grass also appears early, but in much tighter tufts than 'Karl Foerster' has, and the flowering plumes don't appear until August.

Korean feather reed grass is distinctly clump-forming, with an upright but somewhat vase-shaped habit. Unlike 'Karl Foerster', it has some fall foliage color, but its stems and leaves break down quickly and have little or no winter presence.

This species seems to tolerate partial shade better than many true grasses. Both it and 'Karl Foerster' are very forgiving of winter-wet soil, too; little wonder that I rely so heavily on them.

Top: Korean feather reed grass with Japanese maple (*Acer palmatum*), plantain-leaved sedge (*Carex plantaginea*), and 'Blackbird' spurge (*Euphorbia*) [early October]

Above: Korean feather reed grass with Diabolo ninebark (*Physocarpus opulifolius* 'Monlo') [early November]

Echinacea

Purple Coneflowers

Asteraceae
Aster Family

After wasting way too much money on fancy hybrids that fizzle out after just a year or two, I'm sticking with seed-grown purple coneflowers (*Echinacea purpurea*) from now on.

- Full sun to partial shade
- Average, well-drained soil
- 3-4 feet tall; 12-18 inches wide
- Zones 3-9

✓ Multi-season interest
✓ Attracts birds and butterflies

✗ No significant fall color

I think of purple coneflowers (*Echinacea purpurea*) as late-summer perennials, so I'm always surprised to see them budding up in May and often blooming by early June. The big, broad blooms are a welcome sight in my early-summer garden, because I usually don't have much else in bloom at that time.

By the end of June, the other summer perennials are starting to flower too, so there are plenty of other potential companions. If you're a stickler for careful color echoes, though, it can be tricky to choose compatible partners, because purple coneflowers are an unlikely combination of rosy pink "petals" (technically, ray florets) and orangey centers.

Purple coneflowers with 'Red Rubin' basil (*Ocimum basilicum*), and 'Worcester Gold' blue mist shrub (*Caryopteris* x *clandonensis*) [late July]

Burgundy Bedmates

You can't go wrong pairing purple coneflowers with dark-leaved companions. Maroon and burgundy foliage complements the coneflower blooms all season long.

Top left: 'Magnus' purple coneflower with Diabolo ninebark (*Physocarpus opulifolius* 'Monlo'), teasel (*Dipsacus*), red orach (*Atriplex hortensis* 'Rubra'), 'Limerock Ruby' coreopsis, and Japanese blood grass (*Imperata cylindrica* 'Rubra') [mid-July]

Top right: 'Magnus' purple coneflower with 'Carin' Joe-Pye weed (*Eutrochium maculatum*), Fine Wine weigela (*Weigela florida* 'Bramwell'), and 'Rotstrahlbusch' switch grass (*Panicum virgatum*) [late July]

Left: Purple coneflower with golden elderberry (*Sambucus nigra* 'Aurea'), pincushion flower (*Scabiosa atropurpurea*), nasturtium (*Tropaeolum majus*), and 'Purple Knight' alternanthera (*Alternanthera dentata*) [mid-August]

Better Together

Masses of purple coneflowers make a big splash of color in summer borders, bridging the gap between early bloomers and fall-interest perennials and grasses.

To extend their display even longer, I like to shear the front half of each drift in late May or early June. The sheared plants end up being about 1 foot shorter and come into bloom 4 to 6 weeks later than the uncut plants, producing plenty of fresh flowers just as the others are passing their peak.

Top: Purple coneflowers — those in front cut back by half in late May — with 'Lemon Queen' perennial sunflower (*Helianthus*), Knock Out rose (*Rosa* 'Radrazz'), tall ironweed (*Vernonia gigantea*), and 'Cloud Nine' switch grass (*Panicum virgatum*) [mid-August]

Right: Purple coneflowers with golden elderberry (*Sambucus nigra* 'Aurea'), tall ironweed (*Vernonia gigantea*), and orange coneflower (*Rudbeckia fulgida* var. *fulgida*) [late July]

Seedheads above the Rest

I generally don't bother with clipping the dead blooms off of purple coneflowers. Even without deadheading, the bloom period is far longer than that of many perennials

It may take a little while to develop an appreciation for the blackened beauty of the dead stems and seedheads. But really, they look terrific with fall-colored and winter-bleached grasses, and with seedheads of other shapes too.

Top left: Purple coneflower seedheads with 'Fireworks' goldenrod (*Solidago rugosa*) and 'Skyracer' purple moor grass (*Molinia caerulea* subsp. *arundinacea*) [mid-October]

Top right: The same plants two months later [mid-December]

Left: Purple coneflower seedheads with 'Northwind' switch grass (*Panicum virgatum*), Bowman's root (*Gillenia stipulata*), aromatic aster (*Symphyotrichum aromaticum*), and 'Cassian' fountain grass (*Pennisetum alopecuroides*) [mid-October]

The Show Goes On

Purple coneflowers stick around well into winter, far extending their season of interest. Their tall, stiff stems stand up even through deep snows, and the seed-laden heads themselves can support a heavy snow cap.

Finches and a number of other birds enjoy feeding on the seeds and eventually reduce the heads to much smaller cones. The birds don't get everything, though, and the dropped seeds will produce a number of seedlings, further thickening up the patch or providing lots of starts for a new drift.

Top: Purple coneflower seedheads with fountain grass (*Pennisetum alopecuroides*) and aromatic aster (*Symphyotrichum aromaticum*) [late January]

Right: Purple coneflower seedhead [mid-February]

Other Coneflowers

Most of the coneflowers in my garden are of the straight species *Echinacea purpurea*, or of the seed strain 'Magnus'. I've tried many others but have succeeded with few.

One that I enjoy in my meadow is pale purple coneflower (*E. pallida*). It's not nearly as showy or as long-flowering, but its thin, drooping ray florets give it an elegant, delicate appearance.

One of the few hybrids I've had some luck with is Sundown ('Evan Saul'). I like the rich orange of the new flowers; that lasts only a day or two, though (longer when it's cool), and then bleaches to a washy peachy pink. Still, it's great with both dark and chartreuse foliage.

Top: Pale purple coneflower (*Echinacea pallida*) with white false indigo (*Baptisia alba*) seedpods and butterfly weed (*Asclepias tuberosa*) [late June]

Above: Sundown hybrid coneflower ('Evan Saul') with 'Gold Mound' spirea (*Spiraea*) and Diabolo ninebark (*Physocarpus opulifolius* 'Monlo') [mid-July]

Eutrochium

Joe-Pye Weeds
Asteraceae
Aster Family

Sure, Joe-Pye weeds (*Eutrochium*) can seed around freely, but otherwise, there's nothing weedy about these big beauties: they're tall, tough, and great for filling space.

- Full sun to partial shade
- Average to moist soil
- 5-7 feet tall; 2-3 feet wide
- Zones 3 or 4-9

✓ Multi-season interest
✓ Great for adding height

× May self-sow abundantly

Oh, great: I just got used to mentally changing *Eupatorium* to *Eupatoriadelphus,* and now we're supposed to use *Eutrochium*. Whatever you call them, Joe-Pye weeds, such as *Eutrochium fistulosum* and *E. maculatum,* are a familiar sight along rural roadsides and in old fields. Their rosy pink blooms look lovely in gardens too — especially mingling with tall warm-season grasses in naturalistic plantings.

Joe-Pye weeds tolerate dry periods once established, but their leaves may end up brown and crispy if they get too dry. It can be worth watering those in high-visibility areas during dry spells.

Joe-Pye weeds (*Eutrochium maculatum*) that were cut back by half in early June, with 'Lemon Lace' silver lace vine (*Fallopia baldschuanica*), giant coneflower (*Rudbeckia maxima*), and Arkansas bluestar (*Amsonia hubrichtii*) [late August]

Structural Color

Many Joe-Pye weed plants have distinctly dark stems. The leaves are held in whorls, leaving stretches of bare stem exposed between the rings of foliage and providing plenty of opportunities for creating combinations with dark-leaved companions. That way, Joe-Pye weeds can contribute garden interest for months before they even begin to bloom.

Top: Joe-Pye weeds with 'Black Beauty' Orienpet lily (*Lilium* hybrid) and 'Karl Foerster' feather reed grass (*Calamagrostis* x *acutiflora*) [mid-August]

Left: 'Carin' Joe-Pye weed (*Eutrochium maculatum*) with Arkansas bluestar (*Amsonia hubrichtii*), 'Purple Emperor' sedum, and red-leaved rose (*Rosa glauca*) [early July]

Joe-Pyes with Partners

Joe-Pye weeds are usually pink (occasionally white), but the intensity of the pink can vary. Some selections, such as 'Gateway', tend to be a rich, rosy pink; others, like 'Carin', are a lighter pink. All tend to darken to some extent as the blooms age.

At any stage, Joe-Pyes combine well with a variety of other colors, from bright yellows and purples to pinks, whites, and silver, as well as straw- to tan-colored grasses.

Top left: 'Carin' Joe-Pye weed with 'Gooseberry Fool' sedum (*Hylotelephium telephium*) and ironweed (*Vernonia*) [late August]

Top right: 'Gateway' Joe-Pye weed (*E. maculatum*) with orange coneflower (*Rudbeckia fulgida* var. *fulgida*) and ironweed [early September]

Right: Joe-Pye weed with 'Karl Foerster' feather reed grass (*Calamagrostis* × *acutiflora*) [mid-September]

Joe-Pyes, Size-Wise

The biggest challenge in choosing partners is the natural height of most Joe-Pyes, which can be up to 7 feet tall in moist soil. I like to cut my plants back by half of whatever height they're at in late May or early June to keep them more in scale; they end up at 4 to 6 feet tall by late summer.

One Joe-Pye that hasn't needed any pruning here is 'Little Joe', a selection of *Eutrochium dubium*. It's not all that little, still reaching about 5 feet tall, but the stems are sturdy and the clumps are dense without any extra work.

Top: 'Little Joe' Joe-Pye weed with 'Dewey Blue' switch grass (*Panicum amarum*), 'Cassian' fountain grass (*Pennisetum alopecuroides*), and 'Morning Light' miscanthus (*Miscanthus sinensis*) [late August]

Left: 'Little Joe' with Indian grass (*Sorghastrum nutans*) [late August]

33

Carrying On

Joe-Pyes are at their best here from mid-August until early October, but that doesn't mean the show ends when the growing season does. Their fluffy-looking flowerheads turn into even fluffier, velvety brown seedheads.

Left alone, the seeds drop into the garden or blow off within a few weeks. (Sometimes I snip off the seed-laden heads and crumble them into the meadow, where I welcome the seedlings.) The branched framework of the seedheads sticks around for several more months, and the skeletons look wonderful in the winter garden, especially when dusted with snow or glazed with ice.

Top left: Joe-Pye weed seedhead [mid-October]

Top right: Joe-Pye weed seedhead [mid-January]

Right: 'Gateway' Joe-Pye weed [mid-February]

Exploring Eupatoriums

Joe-Pye weeds used to be part of the big genus *Eupatorium*, which has since been split up into a number of other genera.

Still in *Eupatorium* is the white-flowered, summer-blooming hyssop-leaved boneset (*E. hyssopifolium*). Its 1- to 3-foot-tall stems are clad in short, thin leaves and topped with heads of fluffy white flowers from mid- or late summer into fall. It's not a "wow" plant, but it's attractive in naturalistic borders.

Some of the former eupatoriums commonly called snakeroots are now in the genus *Ageratina*. Two of my favorites are *A. altissima* 'Prairie Jewel' and *A. aromatica* 'Jocius' Variegate'. Both have brightly variegated leaves in spring, but their showiest feature is their heads of white flowers atop 5- to 6-foot-tall stems in late summer and fall.

Top: 'Jocius' Variegate' lesser snakeroot (*Ageratina aromatica*) with goldenrod (*Solidago*) and Joe-Pye weed (*Eutrochium maculatum*) [mid-September]

Above: Hyssop-leaved boneset (*Eupatorium hyssopifolium*) with little bluestem (*Schizachyrium scoparium*) and 'Bluebird' smooth aster (*Symphyotrichum laeve*) [early October]

Helianthus

Sunflowers
Asteraceae
Aster Family

Perennial sunflowers have much smaller blooms than annual sunflowers (*Helianthus annuus*), but their abundance makes them just as showy.

- Full sun to light shade
- Adapts to a range of soil conditions
- 5-7 feet tall; 3-4 feet wide
- Zones 3 or 4-9

✓ Bright and colorful for late color

✗ Needs frequent division or thinning

There are many perennial species of *Helianthus* to choose from, but the kind I use most here at Hayefield is 'Lemon Queen', a selection of a natural hybrid between stiff sunflower (*H. pauciflorus* var. *subrhomboideus*) and Jerusalem artichoke (*H. tuberosus*).

Considering how quickly Jerusalem artichokes multiply, it's no surprise how vigorous 'Lemon Queen' can be. It stays in clumps but widens steadily and may get overcrowded in just a few seasons. I divide it every 3 years, or else thin the stems to about 4 inches apart in spring to keep it at its best.

'Lemon Queen' perennial sunflower with orange coneflower (*Rudbeckia fulgida* var. *fulgida*) and 'Northwind' switch grass (*Panicum virgatum*) [late August]

Cutting Remarks

'Lemon Queen' thrives where the soil is moist and fertile, but these ideal conditions can lead to sprawling stems. That's one good reason to shear the clumps back by half to two-thirds in late May or early June: the resulting regrowth tends to be sturdier. Plus, by bloom time, the stems will be a foot or so shorter than usual and more in scale with their partners.

An early summer shearing also delays flowering for several weeks, so the plants will peak in late August instead of July —just in time to light up fall borders.

Top: 'Lemon Queen' perennial sunflower with purple coneflower (*Echinacea purpurea*), orange coneflower (*Rudbeckia fulgida* var. *fulgida*), and Indian grass (*Sorghastrum nutans*) [early September]

Left: 'Lemon Queen' with ironweed (*Vernonia*) and 'Harrington's Pink' New England aster (*Symphyotrichum novae-angliae*) [late August]

Fitting In

'Lemon Queen' perennial sunflower is a gem for filling large spaces, but it can also work in a narrow spot with a combination of yearly division and pruning. Instead of lifting the whole clump, dig out a few pieces (up to about half of the clump) with a shovel in spring. Fill the holes that are left with a mix of soil and compost.

Top: 'Lemon Queen' perennial sunflower with ironweed (*Vernonia*), Briant Rubidor weigela (*Weigela* 'Olympiade'), 'Oehme' palm sedge (*Carex muskingumensis*), Magic Carpet spirea (*Spiraea japonica* 'Walbuma'), and 'Carin' Joe-Pye weed (*Eutrochium maculatum*) [mid-August]

Right: The same border in fall [mid-November]

38

Another Helianthus

'Lemon Queen' is eye-catching in bloom but not very interesting in other seasons. Willow-leaved sunflower (*H. salicifolius*), on the other hand, has a handsome, dense growth habit and attractive, deep green, slender leaves — traits that are especially noticeable on the scaled-down selection 'Low Down', which reaches only 18 inches instead of the species' 5 to 8 feet tall.

'Low Down' has the usual golden yellow flowers of this genus (more intense than the clear yellow of 'Lemon Queen'), and it blooms later — usually September and October. In flower, the tightly branched stems are practically smothered in color; in winter, they hold up for months and look terrific dusted with snow.

Top: 'Low Down' willow-leaved sunflower with American cranberrybush viburnum (*Viburnum opulus* var. *americanum*) [late September]

Above: 'Low Down' with 'Morning Light' miscanthus (*Miscanthus sinensis*) [early October]

Right: 'Low Down' in winter [mid-February]

Heuchera

Heucheras, Alumroots

Saxifragaceae
Saxifrage Family

Heucheras aren't the easiest plants to please, in my experience, but when they're happy with their spot, they can make great foliage accents.

- Full sun to partial shade
- Average to moist but well-drained soil
- About 1 foot tall and wide
- Zones 4–9

✓ Unusual foliage colors and interesting shapes
✓ Attractive through most of the year

✗ Many fizzle out after a season or two
✗ A favorite with voles and mice

In many ways, I think of foliage heucheras as the perennial equivalent of coleus: their dense, mounded habits can make it challenging to combine them gracefully with other plants, but they are useful for adding spots of color as accent plants.

Actually, calling heucheras "perennial" isn't always accurate. They're winter-hardy here, for sure, but hot, humid summers seem to be a problem for many cultivars, and they fade out after a season or two. I've tried over two dozen selections so far; of those, fewer than half survived to the following year, and just a handful made it to a third year. Those sturdy survivors are now some of my favorite foliage plants, and their merits encourage me to keep trying some new introductions.

'Caramel' heuchera with forget-me-nots (*Myosotis sylvatica*) [late May]

Orange All Over

If I could have only one heuchera, it would be 'Caramel'. It has not simply survived; it positively thrives here. This hybrid includes the southern species hairy alumroot (*H. villosa*) in its parentage, which gives it its unusual tolerance for heat and humidity.

Even more exciting is the cool-season color that 'Caramel' brings to the garden. Its new leaves are a rich orange, aging to peach (in a site with morning sun only) or bleaching to yellowish or greenish tan. I've had good luck with some other orange heucheras, too: 'Peach Flambe' and 'Creme Brulee' have been around for several years, and 'Southern Comfort' is a new favorite.

Top left: 'Caramel' heuchera with Arkansas bluestar (*Amsonia hubrichtii*) and pony tail grass (*Stipa tenuissima*) [late October]

Top right: 'Caramel' heuchera' with shrimp plant (*Justicia brandegeeana*) [late September]

Left: 'Peach Flambe' heuchera with 'All Gold' lemon balm (*Melissa officinalis*) [late April]

Other Options

Of the seemingly countless dark-leaved heucheras, the only one that has been durable in nature and dependable for rich color for me is 'Obsidian'. Its glossy, deep purple to near-black foliage holds up all year long. 'Obsidian' looks great with pretty much any other color, but it's especially dramatic with silver- or chartreuse-leaved partners.

None of the colored-foliage heucheras that I've had luck with produce pretty flowers. But I do grow one that has attractive, fuzzy green leaves all year *and* airy cones of white flowers in fall: 'Autumn Bride' hairy alumroot (*H. villosa*). It's a beauty in partly shady sites.

Top: 'Obsidian' heuchera with 'Angelina' sedum (*Sedum rupestre*) [mid-November]

Right: 'Autumn Bride' hairy alumroot (*H. villosa*) with 'Lemon and Lime' sticky germander (*Teucrium viscidum*) and honeywort (*Cerinthe major*) [early July]

Oh, No – Voles!

Once you get a heuchera established, it's heartbreaking to go out one day and find it flattened. A sudden, dramatic wilt like this usually isn't due to a lack of water; more likely, it's caused by crown damage.

Black vine weevil and strawberry root weevil larvae tunnel through and eat roots and crowns, producing wilt symptoms mostly in late summer and fall. I've very seldom had this problem here, fortunately.

A big problem that I do have is voles. They're most active here in winter and spring, eating entire crowns and leaving the top of the plant unattached. I've had good luck treating the remaining pieces like cuttings, snipping the larger leaves off each piece and sticking the mini-plants in moist potting soil. They usually root quickly, so I can use them to replace the original clump.

Top: Wilted 'Caramel' heuchera clump

Above: 'Caramel' heuchera tops after crown was eaten by voles (note visible tunnel)

43

Molinia

Purple Moor Grasses

Poaceae
Grass Family

The "purple" in purple moor grasses comes from the tiny flowers, and it's not that noticeable. "Golden moor grasses" might be a more appropriate name, due to the glorious golden fall color.

- Full sun to partial shade
- Average to moist but well-drained soil
- 6-8 feet tall; 2-3 feet wide
- Zones 4-9

✓ Tall and graceful appearance
✓ Outstanding fall color

✗ Little winter presence

When we choose a plant for our gardens, we mostly think about how it looks, and maybe how it smells or (even less often for ornamentals) how it tastes. Two traits we rarely consider are how it sounds and how it feels, mainly because few plants are particularly noteworthy in those ways.

Purple moor grass (*Molinia caerulea* subsp. *arundinacea*) is one of those special plants that is magnificent for converting wind into movement and sound: a gentle rustling that's pleasing for screening noises around sitting areas. It's also a pleasure to brush your hands along the slender but wiry flowering stems.

'Skyracer' purple moor grass with aromatic aster (*Symphyotrichum oblongifolium*) [mid-October]

Perfect Partners

It's easy to work small, spring-blooming bulbs into borders because their leaves wither away by the time their perennial partners fill out to cover their space. Taller, later-blooming bulbs — particularly the ultra-showy, large-flowered alliums or ornamental onions (*Allium*) — provide more of a challenge. The alliums' broad, strappy leaves can smother small companions, then leave a big empty space when they go dormant in June. Purple moor grasses grow at just the right rate to let the allium leaves get sun in spring and then fill in once the bulb foliage is finished for the season. They combine well with lilies too.

Top: 'Bergfreund' purple moor grass with 'Stormy Seas' heuchera, 'White Giant' allium, 'Powis Castle' artemisia, and 'Sutherland Gold' elderberry (*Sambucus racemosa*) [late May]

Left: 'Bergfreund' purple moor grass with Sunshine Blue bluebeard (*Caryopteris incana* 'Jason') and 'Sutherland Gold' elderberry [mid-June]

Worth Waiting For

Purple moor grasses are generally classified as cool-season grasses, but they don't begin to flower until mid- to late summer. The tall stems and airy plumes create a misty, see-through screen.

Purple moor grasses also produce fantastic fall color, another trait that's unusual among cool-season grasses. They age through orange and eventually bleach to tan. They typically maintain their form into early winter and then gradually disintegrate. It's a snap to clean up any remaining top growth in spring; just pull it off with your hand — no need for shears.

Top: 'Skyracer' purple moor grass with aromatic aster (*Symphyotrichum oblongifolium*) and 'Sheffield Pink' chrysanthemum [late October]

Right: 'Bergfreund' purple moor grass with 'Angelina' sedum (*Sedum rupestre*) and 'Powis Castle' artemisia [mid-November]

Considering Spodiopogon

Like purple moor grasses, frost grass (*Spodiopogon sibiricus*) — also known as Siberian graybeard and silver spike grass — falls somewhere between cool- and warm-season grasses. It too starts flowering in midsummer, reaching 5 to 6 feet tall, and it too can have striking fall color (deep red at its best, though it's more often a plummy brown here).

Overall, frost grass has a fairly dense habit, with foliage that's more stiffly horizontal than arching, but it can make a pleasing rustling noise when the weather is breezy. It holds up into early winter, at least, then starts to break down and is mostly gone by early spring.

Frost grass thrives in full sun to light shade in evenly moist soil in Zones 5 to 8.

Top: Frost grass with orange coneflower (*Rudbeckia fulgida* var. *fulgida*) [mid-August]

Above: Frost grass with southern bush honeysuckle (*Diervilla sessilifolia*) [mid-October]

Right: Frost grass with 'Cassian' fountain grass (*Pennisetum alopecuroides*), orange coneflower, and purple coneflower (*Echinacea purpurea*) [mid-December]

47

Panicum

Switch Grasses

Poaceae
Grass Family

It's hard to think of anything bad to say about switch grasses (*Panicum virgatum*). They're about as low-maintenance as you can get.

- Full sun to light shade
- Adapt to a range of soil conditions
- 4-8 feet tall; 1-2 feet wide
- Zones 2-9

✓ Summer, fall, and winter interest
✓ Outstanding fall color

✗ May flop in rich soil, or if crowded

The fact that switch grasses are native to nearly every state in the U.S. — and much of Canada, too — gives you some idea of how tough and adaptable they are. Planted singly, these clump-forming perennials make striking vertical accents; in drifts, they are excellent for adding height, movement, and multi-season interest to borders.

Best of all, there's a large number of named switch grass cultivars to choose from, varying in height, habit, texture, and summer and fall foliage colors, so there's at least one selection to complement companions in just about any sunny site.

'Dallas Blues' switch grass with aromatic aster (*Symphyotrichum oblongifolium*) and the seedheads of orange coneflower (*Rudbeckia fulgida* var. *fulgida*) [early October]

Use the Blues

'Dallas Blues' is distinctly different from other *P. virgatum* cultivars, with much wider leaf blades in a bright but cool powder blue. It has a sturdily upright to vase-shaped habit, reaching 6 to 7 feet at the tips of its airy, pink flower plumes. And, its fall foliage color is a clear yellow, aging to a coppery brown that holds up all through the winter. If you have room for only one big grass, this is the one to try!

Top left: 'Dallas Blues' with 'Becky' Shasta daisy (*Leucanthemum*) and southernwood (*Artemisia abrotanum*) [late June]

Top right: 'Dallas Blues' with orange coneflower (*Rudbeckia fulgida*) seedheads [late October]

Left: 'Dallas Blues' with orange coneflower and Japanese emperor oak (*Quercus dentata*) [early February]

A Touch of Red

It's not unusual for some of the medium-sized, green-leaved switch grasses to take on reddish tinges as the growing season progresses. For a while, 'Shenandoah' was about the earliest, turning reddish in mid- to late summer. Now there are cultivars that start coloring in early summer, such as 'Huron Solstice' and 'Prairie Fire'. All of these reach about 4 feet tall.

Top left: 'Shenandoah' switch grass with giant fleeceflower (*Persicaria polymorpha*) and 'Lemon Lace' silver fleece vine (*Fallopia baldschuanica*) [early July]

Top right: 'Shenandoah' with northern sea oats (*Chasmanthium latifolium*), Tiger Eyes sumac (*Rhus typhina* 'Bailtiger'), and aromatic aster (*Symphyotrichum oblongifolium*) [late September]

Right: 'Shenandoah' with frost aster (*S. pilosum*), Joe-Pye weed (*Eutrochium maculatum*), and aromatic aster [early October]

An Upright Character

'Heavy Metal' is one of the older cultivars, but it's still a good one for blue-green foliage. It reaches 4 to 5 feet tall in bloom. The growth habit is strongly upright for the first few years but loosens up as the clumps expand. Dividing the clumps every 3 to 5 years keeps them looking their best. As with most switch grasses, the fall color and winter structure of 'Heavy Metal' are outstanding.

Top left: 'Heavy Metal' switch grass with purple milkweed (*Asclepias purpurascens*), 'Bluebird' smooth aster (*Symphyotrichum laeve*), and 'Waterlily' autumn crocus (*Colchicum*) [late September]

Top right: 'Heavy Metal' with purple milkweed, aromatic aster (*S. oblongifolium*), three-flowered maple (*Acer triflorum*), and cut-leaved staghorn sumac (*Rhus typhina* 'Laciniata') [early October]

Left: 'Heavy Metal' on ice [mid-December]

Straight and Narrow

When I need a plant that's tall but don't have a lot of ground space for it, 'Northwind' switch grass is one of my top choices. It reaches 6 to 7 feet tall in bloom but just about 1 foot wide at the base, with a strongly vertical habit. It gets somewhat wider and more vase-shaped after 4 or 5 years (sooner if the soil is rich and moist), but so far, I've never had older clumps flop, even under the weight of winter snow and ice.

Top left: 'Northwind' switch grass with giant coneflower (*Rudbeckia maxima*) [mid-July]

Top right: 'Northwind' with aromatic aster (*Symphyotrichum oblongifolium*), 'Cassian' fountain grass (*Pennisetum alopecuroides*), orange coneflower (*Rudbeckia fulgida* var. *fulgida*), and Bowman's root (*Gillenia stipulata*) [mid-October]

Right: 'Northwind' in winter [mid-February]

Another Panicum

Most of the switch grasses that are readily available to gardeners are cultivars of *Panicum virgatum*, but there's one that's a little different: 'Dewey Blue', a selection of *P. amarum*. The foliage is a bright gray-blue, though what I like even better are the lacy-looking, nodding flower- and seedheads.

Bitter switch grass is native to coastal areas but grows well even in heavier conditions. In fact, I find that 'Dewey Blue' seeds around much more freely than the ordinary switch grass around here. It is, however, much more prone to flopping in moist, fertile soils than the dry, sandy conditions it's naturally adapted to. To deal with that, I like to put it at the middle or back of a border where it can lean on sturdier companions.

Top: 'Dewey Blue' bitter switch grass (*Panicum amarum*) with purple coneflower (*Echinacea purpurea*) [mid-July]

Above: 'Dewey Blue' with golden lace (*Patrinia scabiosifolia*), 'Karl Foerster' feather reed grass (*Calamagrostis* x *acutiflora*), and orange coneflower (*Rudbeckia fulgida* var. *fulgida*) [late August]

Right: 'Dewey Blue' (at back left) with 'The Blues' little bluestem (*Schizachyrium scoparium*), orange coneflower, and 'Karl Foerster' feather reed grass [early November]

Patrinia

Patrinias
Valerianaceae
Valerian Family

It might be hard to get excited about yet another yellow perennial for fall. But golden lace (*Patrinia scabiosifolia*) is a beauty that's well worth hunting for.

- Full sun to light shade
- Adapts to a range of soil conditions
- 5-6 feet tall; 12-18 inches wide
- Zones 5-8

✓ Bright lemon yellow blooms
✓ Showy fall foliage and stem color

✗ May self-sow

Why isn't this great perennial more popular? Well, for one, golden lace has the same "problem" as many other late-season bloomers: it's an ordinary-looking clump of green foliage before it flowers, and it's not eye-catching in a pot during the spring plant-shopping frenzy. It also seems to be a little difficult to transplant unless it's small.

Yet another issue is that patrinias can be alternate hosts for a rust fungus that attacks daylilies (*Hemerocallis*). Details are still sketchy, but for now, some daylily aficionados prefer to keep patrinias out of their garden.

Golden lace (*Patrinia scabiosifolia*) [late August]

Amazing Lace

None of the reasons I can think of for golden lace's lack of popularity discourage me from growing it. In fact, I'm thrilled that it has finally gotten to the point of self-sowing here.

Despite its common name, golden lace isn't really golden: it's more of a greenish yellow — a nice change from the brassy yellows of goldenrods (*Solidago*). The flat-topped umbels and the tiered placement of the bloom clusters add a different form, too.

Top: Golden lace with goldenrod (*Solidago*), ironweeds (*Vernonia*) and Joe-Pye weed (*Eutrochium maculatum*) [late August]

Left: Golden lace with fountain grass (*Pennisetum alopecuroides*), orange coneflower (*Rudbeckia fulgida* var. *fulgida*), and silver willow (*Salix alba* var. *sericea*) [late August]

The Show Goes On

Golden lace begins blooming in late summer (usually around mid-August) and continues well into fall. In fact, it can still be flowering when the fall color develops. The stems typically turn deep red, while the leaves take on glowing shades of red and orange. The show is especially striking when paired with the golden yellow fall color of Arkansas bluestar (*Amsonia hubrichtii*).

After frost, golden lace's bloom stalks hang around for a month or two, looking great dusted with snow or sparking with ice.

Top left: Golden lace with aromatic aster (*Symphyotrichum oblongifolium*) and New England aster (*S. novae-angliae*) [late September]

Top right: Golden lace fall color [late October]

Right: Golden lace on ice [mid-December]

Going for Gold

Before I was able to get golden lace established, my go-to perennial for fall yellow was 'Fireworks' goldenrod (*Solidago rugosa*), and it's still one of my favorite late bloomers. It comes into flower several weeks later — typically the first or second week of September — and keeps going through October.

One great thing about 'Fireworks' is that it's a clump-former. It expands over time, but not in a troublesome way, and dividing the clumps every 3 years gives plenty of starts for new plantings. Also, the horizontal branching of the upper part of the stems does a good job weaving the clump together, so staking isn't an issue. After its long bloom period, 'Fireworks' dries beautifully in place and holds its form well through the winter — a bonus season of interest.

Top: 'Fireworks' goldenrod with golden lace (*Patrinia scabiosifolia*), ironweed (*Vernonia*), fountain grass (*Pennisetum alopecuroides*), and 'Fireworks' globe amaranth (*Gomphrena*) [mid-September]

Above: 'Fireworks' goldenrod with orange coneflower (*Rudbeckia fulgida* var. *fulgida*) [mid-September]

Pennisetum

Fountain Grasses

**Poaceae
Grass Family**

Fountain grass (*Pennisetum alopecuroides*) may be rather common, but it's also sturdy and dependable.

- Full sun to light shade
- Average to moist soil
- 2-3 feet tall and wide
- Zones 5-9

✓ Brushy flower and seed spikes
✓ Outstanding winter form

× May self-sow

There are plenty of gorgeous tall grasses, but options for the front of the border are much more limited, especially if you want a clump-former, and one with multi-season interest too.

Prairie dropseed (*Sporobolus heterolepis*) is one compact grass that I like very much, because it has excellent orange fall color, and the dried foliage lasts well through the winter. Fountain grasses have much denser flower and seed spikes, though, creating more of a show from late summer into winter. Plus, they don't have the weird cilantro-like scent that prairie dropseed has when in bloom.

Fountain grass with 'Fireworks' goldenrod (*Solidago rugosa*), aromatic aster (*Symphyotrichum oblongifolium*), Brazilian vervain (*Verbena bonariensis*), silver willow (*Salix alba* var. *sericea*), and 'Heavenly Blue' morning glory (*Ipomoea tricolor*) [late September]

Late-Summer Splendor

Here in southeastern Pennsylvania, fountain grasses send up their fluffy flower spikes around mid-August, just in time to mingle with many other later-blooming perennials and grasses. They grow well in somewhat heavy soil and seem to prefer regular rainfall, but they also tolerate our usual summer dry spells just fine, putting on a splendid show even without watering.

Top: 'Cassian' fountain grass with frost grass (*Spodiopogon sibiricus*), 'Skyracer' purple moor grass (*Molinia caerulea* subsp. *arundinacea*), and aromatic aster (*Symphyotrichum oblongifolium*) [early October]

Left: Fountain grass with Brazilian vervain (*Verbena bonariensis*), 'Fireworks' goldenrod (*Solidago rugosa*), golden lace (*Patrinia scabiosifolia*), and 'Alma Potschke' New England aster (*Symphyotrichum novae-angliae*) [mid-September]

Persistence is a Virtue

One of the best investments I made when I started the gardens here at Hayefield was a dozen pots of 'Cassian' fountain grass. Over the years, I've divided them many times and used them to fill many areas.

'Cassian' reaches just about 2 feet tall and wide, so it's excellent as an edging for a large border. The yellow fall color is outstanding, too, and the bleached seedheads last into December, or until the birds pick them apart.

Top: 'Cassian' fountain grass with 'Skyracer' purple moor grass (*Molinia caerulea* subsp. *arundinacea*) and Arkansas bluestar (*Amsonia hubrichtii*) [late October]

Right: 'Cassian' fountain grass with orange coneflower (*Rudbeckia fulgida* var. *fulgida*) seedheads, frost grass (*Spodiopogon sibiricus*), purple coneflower (*Echinacea purpurea*) seedheads, and Arkansas bluestar [mid-November]

Another Pennisetum

Grasses have many great qualities, but colorful flowers isn't one of them. One exception is 'Karley Rose' Oriental fountain grass (*Pennisetum orientale*). To be fair, it's not *much* of an exception, because it's not a very strong color, but it *is* a hazy pink in bloom: enough to make it an elegant echo for other pink summer flowers, and for soft yellows and purples too. The slender spikes age to light tan for fall, then bleach out further through late autumn.

Structurally, Oriental fountain grass isn't as sturdy as the usual species: it tends to sprawl in rainy weather, especially if the soil is rich, and you'll probably want to cut it down in December because it looks rather messy in winter. But for all its faults, 'Karley Rose' sure is a pretty sight in summer borders.

Top: 'Karley Rose' with Joe-Pye weed (*Eutrochium maculatum*), tall ironweed (*Vernonia gigantea*), golden elderberry (*Sambucus nigra* 'Aurea'), and purple coneflower (*Echinacea purpurea*) [early August]

Above: 'Karley Rose' Oriental fountain grass with 'Frau Dagmar Hastrup' rose and Arkansas bluestar (*Amsonia hubrichtii*) [early August]

Right: 'Karley Rose' with the dried stalks of Joe-Pye weed and 'Cloud Nine' switch grass (*Panicum virgatum*) [mid-November]

Persicaria

Fleeceflowers

Polygonaceae
Buckwheat Family

It's a pity that so many gardeners are scared to plant fleeceflowers (*Persicaria*), because some of the species are perfectly well-behaved clump-formers.

- Full sun to light shade
- Adapt to a range of soil conditions
- Size varies by species
- Zones 4 or 5-9

✓ Showy summer plumes or spikes
✓ Long-lived even without division

× A favorite with Japanese beetles

As a group, fleeceflowers — also known as knotweeds — tend to have a reputation for being nightmarishly spreading thugs, due to a few bad apples in the bunch: especially Japanese knotweed (*Polygonum cuspidatum*). The lovely garden fleeceflowers used to be in the same genus, and some of them look similar to the invasive kind, so they get tarred with the same brush. Sure, the good guys can get big too, but they don't creep all over creation, and they're not self-sowing menaces either. Give them the space they need, and they won't give you any trouble.

Giant fleeceflower (*Persicaria polymorpha*) with little bluestem (*Schizachyrium scoparium*), purple coneflower (*Echinacea purpurea*), 'Lemon Queen' perennial sunflower (*Helianthus*), and 'Cloud Nine' switch grass (*Panicum virgatum*) [mid-August]

Not for the Small Garden

Giant fleeceflower (*Persicaria polymorpha*) is one of my favorite perennials, though really, it acts more like a shrub, easily reaching 6 feet tall and wide each year. Plant annuals around it for the first few years, or else plan to move its partners out of the way as it fills out.

Giant fleeceflower is exceptional as a background plant, or with large drifts of other perennials in a border. It makes a superb partner for shrubs and trees, too.

Top left: Giant fleeceflower with Knock Out rose (*Rosa* 'Radrazz') [mid-June]

Top right: Giant fleeceflower with silver willow (*Salix alba* var. *sericea*) and pony tail grass (*Stipa tenuissima*) [mid-June]

Left: Giant fleeceflower with 'Karl Foerster' feather reed grass (*Calamagrostis* x *acutiflora*) and 'Center Glow' ninebark (*Physocarpus opulifolius*) [mid-June]

Ten Months of Magnificence

Giant fleeceflower starts blooming in mid- to late May here in southeastern Pennsylvania, when it's just 2 to 3 feet tall, and it's in full fluffy white glory in June and July. Eventually, the plumes turn pinkish and then drop off to leave brown skeletons. The bright green foliage can show bright red to rich maroon fall color before it too turns brown. The dark, sturdy stalks remain standing through the winter, creating an interesting presence when dusted with snow or encased in ice.

Top: The same border that's shown on page 62, with Japanese emperor oak (*Quercus dentata*) [mid-November]

Right: Giant fleeceflower coated with ice [mid-December]

Big and Beautiful

Here's another case where mixed-up nomenclature scares gardeners away from a perfectly good plant. I acquired 'Crimson Beauty' as a *Persicaria* hybrid, but I've also seen it sold under *Fallopia japonica* and *Polygonum cuspidatum*: the same names applied to the invasive Japanese knotweed.

'Crimson Beauty' does look like a pink-flowered version of that scary weed, with one huge difference: it's a clump-former, not a rampant spreader. It does get large, though — 6 to 8 feet tall and wide — so be sure to give it plenty of room.

Top: 'Crimson Beauty' fleeceflower with 'Jocius' Variegate' lesser snakeroot (*Ageratina aromatica*) and silver willow (*Salix alba* var. *sericea*) [mid-October]

Left: 'Crimson Beauty' fleeceflower mingling with Virginia creeper (*Parthenocissus quinquefolia*) [mid-October]

Late-Season Spikes

Mountain fleeceflower (*P. amplexicaulis*) is more of a spreader than a clumper, but not to the point of being aggressive. Digging up some of the excess every few years keeps the clumps a fine size for a border and gives welcome starts for new patches.

The 3- to 4-foot-tall, rosy red spikes add welcome color to the late summer and fall garden, and they combine well with just about any rich color, except maybe scarlet reds.

Top left: 'Taurus' mountain fleeceflower with 'Isla Gold' tansy (*Tanacetum vulgare*) [early August]

Top right: 'Taurus' mountain fleeceflower with Tropicanna canna (*Canna* 'Phaison') and an orange chrysanthemum [early September]

Right: 'Taurus' mountain fleeceflower with 'Profusion Orange' zinnia, goldenrod (*Solidago*), and purple fountain grass (*Pennisetum setaceum* 'Rubrum') [early October]

Another Persicaria

I'm not a big fan of short plants in general, but dwarf or Himalayan fleeceflower (*Persicaria affinis*) has found its way into my plantings because of its many good qualities. When it starts flowering in July, the soft pink new blooms are most evident, but as they age to a deep pinkish red, the 6- to 12-inch-tall spikes blend more readily with the reds, oranges, purples, and yellows of the late summer and fall garden. The rich red autumn foliage color is also outstanding.

Dwarf fleeceflower does spread a bit once it gets settled in, but it mostly creeps on top of the ground, so you don't have to worry about it sneaking around and popping up through other plants. And, it's easy enough to pull out if you get too much.

Top: 'Dimity' dwarf fleeceflower with Arkansas bluestar (*Amsonia hubrichtii*) [late July]

Above: 'Dimity' dwarf fleeceflower with Japanese blood grass (*Imperata cylindrica* 'Rubra') [early October]

Right: 'Dimity' dwarf fleeceflower with Arkansas bluestar [mid-November]

Rudbeckia

Orange Coneflowers

Asteraceae
Aster Family

Orange coneflowers (*Rudbeckia fulgida*) may be utterly common, but they're also sturdy and fuss-free.

- Full sun to light shade
- Average, well-drained soil
- 24-30 inches tall; about 1 foot wide
- Zones 3 or 4-9

✓ Showy flowers for late summer and early fall
✓ Long-lasting seedheads provide winter interest and seeds for birds

✗ May self-sow freely

I used to consider orange coneflowers — also known as black-eyed Susans — to be boring and overplanted, mostly in the form of summer-blooming 'Goldsturm' (*Rudbeckia fulgida* var. *sullivantii*). Seriously, they were **everywhere**!

But when I started the gardens here at Hayefield, I was desperate for cheery, easy-care color, and I bought a flat of *R. fulgida* var. *fulgida* to use as fillers. Blooming about a month later than 'Goldsturm' — or even later, with a bit of pruning — they've won my heart with their bright faces and trouble-free nature. Good thing, because I now have a whole lot of them.

Orange coneflowers (*Rudbeckia fulgida* var. *fulgida*) with 'Big Ears' lamb's ears (*Stachys byzantina*) [late August]

Late-Season Sunshine

The variety *fulgida* typically starts flowering in late July or early August here in southeastern Pennsylvania, and it continues into early fall. I like to delay the bloom even longer, so I shear the clumps back by about half in early June. The plants then start flowering in mid- to late August and look fresh through September, or even longer. They also end up a bit shorter: more like 18 to 22 inches instead of the usual 24 to 30 inches tall.

Top: Orange coneflower (*R. fulgida* var. *fulgida*) with 'Rotstrahlbusch' switch grass (*Panicum virgatum*) [late August]

Left: Orange coneflower with fountain grass (*Pennisetum alopecuroides*), 'Fireworks' globe amaranth (*Gomphrena*), and 'Bluebird' smooth aster (*Symphyotrichum laeve*) [late September]

Heads Up

Even better than orange coneflowers' abundant blooms are the sturdy, long-lasting seedheads. The dark-dotted clumps look great with rich fall foliage colors as well as with bleached, brown, or russet, dried grasses through the winter. Many birds relish the seeds as winter food, but plenty of the seeds will drop, too, so if you leave the seedheads, expect seedlings.

Top left: Orange coneflower with 'Cassian' fountain grass (*Pennisetum alopecuroides*) [mid-October]

Top right: Orange coneflower with 'Dallas Blues' switch grass (*Panicum virgatum*) and Japanese emperor oak (*Quercus dentata*) [mid-November]

Right: Orange coneflower with little bluestem (*Schizachyrium scoparium*) [mid-December]

Another Rudbeckia

Orange coneflowers have showy flowers and interesting seedheads, but their foliage isn't especially interesting. Giant coneflower (*Rudbeckia maxima*) is a different story, with broad, powder-blue leaves that form hosta-like clumps in spring, later rising on the 6- to 8-foot-tall bloom stalks.

After the mid- to late July bloom peak, large seedheads form and last well into fall. Finches and other birds usually devour the dark seeds by early winter, but the pointed cores of the seedheads remain, and the tall stems stand for another month or two, at least.

Giant coneflower is tall enough for the back of a border, but it also looks great near the front or next to a path, where you can admire the beautiful leaves close up.

Top: Giant coneflower [early July]

Above: Giant coneflower with northern sea oats (*Chasmanthium latifolium*) [mid-July]

Right: Giant coneflower with 'Morning Light' miscanthus (*Miscanthus sinensis*) and 'Saratoga' ginkgo (*Ginkgo biloba*) [early October]

Sanguisorba

Burnets
Rosaceae
Rose Family

Why did I take so long to catch on to the beauty of burnets? Maybe because they're not widely available for sale. They've certainly been worth searching for.

- Full sun to light shade
- Average, well-drained soil
- 4-6 feet tall; 12-18 inches wide
- Zones 4-9

✓ Unique bloom form
✓ Late-summer and fall flower color

✗ May need support when young

For many years, I knew burnets only as the herb commonly called salad burnet (*Sanguisorba minor* or *Poterium sanguisorba*), with pretty, ferny foliage but uninteresting flowers just about 1 foot tall. Then, in Piet Oudolf's books, I saw some of the much taller species and was intrigued with their unusual flower forms and rich colors.

I finally found the white- and purple-flowered forms of Japanese burnet (*S. tenuifolia*) through mail-order nurseries. They weren't impressive for the first few years — rather scrawny and sprawly, in fact — but since they settled in, they've been magnificent.

Purple Japanese burnet (*Sanguisorba tenuifolia* 'Purpurea') with 'Coppelia' sneezeweed (*Helenium*) [late August]

Airy Elegance

The dark blooms of purple Japanese burnet show up best against a light-colored background: green is okay, but yellow flowers or leaves are even better.

It's difficult to stake young burnets gracefully, but Y-stakes can work to prop them up if necessary. After 4 or 5 years, the clumps seem to stand up just fine on their own. Or, try cutting the stems back by a third to a half in June to keep them a bit lower and sturdier.

Top: Purple Japanese burnet against golden elderberry (*Sambucus nigra* 'Aurea') with 'Lemon Queen' perennial sunflower (*Helianthus*) [late August]

Left: Purple Japanese burnet with 'Coppelia' sneezeweed (*Helenium*) and tall ironweed (*Vernonia gigantea*) [late August]

A Nod to White

In many ways, white Japanese burnet (*S. tenuifolia* 'Alba') is just like the purple version: It forms similar clumps of deep green, ferny foliage; it reaches to about 6 feet tall; and it too can produce beautiful fall leaf colors. Its flowers are rather different, though: they're white (as you may guess from the name), fluffy-looking, and nodding instead of upright.

Top left: White burnet foliage with giant fleeceflower (*Persicaria polymorpha*) and groundseltree (*Baccharis halimifolia*) [late June]

Top right: White Japanese burnet with 'Little Joe' Joe-Pye weed (*Eutrochium dubium*) and aromatic aster (*Symphyotrichum oblongifolium*) [mid-August]

Right: White Japanese burnet fall foliage with aromatic aster [mid-October]

Other Sanguisorbas

Once you experience one burnet, it's tempting to hunt down others to try. A few years ago, I found 'Tanna', a selection of *Sanguisorba officinalis*. It's much shorter than Japanese burnet — to just about 18 inches — and flowers earlier (in mid- to late summer). It's not especially eye-catching but does add an interesting flower form and nice ferny foliage to the front of a border.

One that's even more ornamental is the variegated selection 'Dali Marble'. It is sold as a cultivar of *S. menziesii,* even though that species usually flowers in late spring to early summer and this one blooms in late summer or fall. 'Dali Marble' has a thin cream to white margin on each wavy-edged leaflet, forming a showy clump of foliage well before the deep purple-red flowers bloom atop 3- to 4-foot-tall stems.

Top: 'Tanna' burnet (*Sanguisorba officinalis* 'Tanna') with purple fountain grass (*Pennisetum setaceum* 'Rubrum') [mid-July]

Above: 'Dali Marble' burnet (*S. menziesii*) with blue flax (*Linum perenne*) [mid-May]

Right: 'Dali Marble' against aromatic aster (*Symphyotrichum oblongifolium*) [mid-October]

Stachys

Lamb's Ears

Lamiaceae
Mint Family

Lamb's ears (*Stachys byzantina*) may be kind of old-fashioned as perennials go, but they're still useful for their silvery to gray-green color and bold foliage texture.

- Full sun to shade
- Average, well-drained soil
- 6-8 inches tall; 12-18 inches wide
- Zones 3-9

✓ Velvety, silvery foliage
✓ Spreads, but not uncontrollably

× Foliage may rot in sultry summers
× Flowering stems tend to sprawl

It's hard to resist petting the velvety foliage of lamb's ears: it's just so soft and velvety. It's a pleasure to work around the plants, or to brush by them on the edge of a path. They do have some faults, though: their patches can expand rather quickly, they look untidy in bloom, and they tend to "melt out" in heat and humidity.

Over the years, I've had an on-again, off-again fondness for the selection 'Big Ears' (also sold as 'Helene von Stein'). Sometimes I get tired of the summer rot, but I've found that if I shear all of the foliage back to about an inch in early June, it grows back quickly and doesn't seem to go limp in summer. And really, it's one of the few silvery plants that don't seem to mind moist, fertile soil.

'Big Ears' lamb's ears with autumn crocus (*Colchicum autumnale*) [late September]

High Contrast Combos

The leaves of regular lamb's ears are usually a bright silver-white, while those of 'Big Ears' tend to be more of a silvery gray (especially when new, or in cool weather) to gray-green. Either way, they make striking contrasts with reds, deep purples, and blacks. Pairing them with dark-leaved plants that have strongly upright, strappy or grassy foliage adds a contrast of form as well as color.

Top left: 'Big Ears' with 'Oakhurst' pineapple lily (*Eucomis comosa*) and 'Purple Emperor' sedum [late June]

Top right: Frosted 'Big Ears' with 'Persian Chocolate' loosestrife (*Lysimachia congestiflora*) [late October]

Left: 'Big Ears' with Japanese blood grass (*Imperata cylindrica* 'Rubra') [late October]

77

Soft and Subtle

Lamb's ears look as soft as they feel, making beautiful partners for pastel pinks and purples, and blues, too. They're also lovely with bright yellow, blue, or green foliage.

When they bloom, lamb's ears have tiny pinkish flowers on the woolly spikes. They can be pretty when fresh, but if you don't like them, simply snip them off.

Top left: 'Big Ears' lamb's ears with Joe-Pye weed (*Eutrochium maculatum*) and 'Karl Foerster' feather reed grass (*Calamagrostis* x *acutiflora*) [mid-August]

Top right: 'Big Ears' flowering stalks with 'Caradonna' salvia [late May]

Right: Lamb's ears with 'Loraine Sunshine' ox-eye (*Heliopsis helianthoides*), sea kale (*Crambe maritima*), and 'Snow Fairy' bluebeard (*Caryopteris incana*) [mid-August]

Other Stachys

Unlike lamb's ears, wood betony (*Stachys officinalis*, also sold as *S. betonica*) is known best for its late-spring and early-summer flowers. The short, plump spikes look much like a sort of sage (*Salvia*), but instead of blooming in shades of purple-blue, they're a slightly purplish pink (in the species), soft pink (in 'Rosea'), or bright white (in 'Alba').

Sometimes I leave on the 12- to 16-inch-tall flowering stems after the blooms drop, to let the plants self-sow. But usually I shear them off, which encourages the plants to put on a flush of fresh leafy growth. (The small, scalloped-edged, deep green leaves form dense rosettes that look good well into winter.) I've heard that the clumps may eventually spread to form a ground cover, but mine have stayed in distinct clumps for many years.

Top: Wood betony (*Stachys officinalis*) with larkspur (*Consolida ambigua*) and angelica (*Angelica archangelica*) [late June]

Above: White wood betony (*S. officinalis* 'Alba') with sea holly (*Eryngium*) [late June]

Stipa

Pony Tail Grasses

Poaceae
Grass Family

If I had to choose just one grass to grow, pony tail grass (*Stipa tenuissima*, a.k.a. *Nassella tenuissima*) would probably be my top pick.

- Full sun to light shade
- Average, well-drained soil
- 12-18 inches tall; 8-12 inches wide
- Zones 5 or 6-9

✓ Graceful, arching habit
✓ Essentially year-round interest

✗ May rot out in wet conditions

When I first started growing pony tail grass, also known as Mexican feather grass, it died out every winter, so I had to start new plants from seed each spring. Over the last few years, though, it has become more reliably perennial, to the point that I can divide the clumps each spring to expand my plantings. I've heard that it can overwinter even in Zone 5 if it's in very well-drained soil.

Pony tail grass also self-sows a bit, providing additional starter plants. Maybe that will become a problem at some point, but for now, I can't imagine having too much of this beautiful cool-season grass.

Pony tail grass (*Stipa tenuissima*) [mid-June]

Multi-Season Magic

Pony tail grass has a presence about 50 weeks of the year, making it one of the hardest-working perennials in the garden. I usually cut it to 2 to 3 inches in early to mid-April, and new green growth rises within a week or so.

The tiny green flowers bloom in June and mature to golden seedheads in July. The seeds can be so abundant that the clumps weigh down the slender stems. I comb out the clumps with my fingers to harvest the seeds and remove the excess weight.

Top: Pony tail grass with Brazilian vervain (*Verbena bonariensis*), 'Silver and Gold' yellow-twig dogwood (*Cornus sericea*), and 'Profusion White' zinnia [late July]

Left: Pony tail grass with 'Silver and Gold' yellow-twig dogwood and New England aster (*Symphyotrichum novae-angliae*) [late September]

Everlasting Elegance

Beautiful in itself, pony tail grass also has a special way of interacting with the conditions around it. The slender foliage sways in the slightest breeze, and the feathery blond seedheads are absolutely magical when backlit by the rising or setting sun.

For such a delicate-looking grass, the foliage is amazingly durable, looking lovely in winter when traced with frost, dusted with snow, or outlined in ice.

Top left: Pony tail grass with 'Edith Wolford' bearded iris and 'Screamin' Yellow' false indigo (*Baptisia sphaerocarpa*) [early June]

Top right: Pony tail grass with Harvest Moon purple coneflower [*Echinacea* 'Matthew Saul') [late July]

Right: Pony tail grass with 'Cardinal' red-twig dogwood (*Cornus sericea*) [mid-December]

82

A Stipa Substitute

If you're looking for a fine-textured, multi-season grass but would prefer one that's dependably perennial all the way to Zone 3, consider prairie dropseed (*Sporobolus heterolepis*). Its foliage is more arching than that of pony tail grass, it forms more rounded mounds, and it is a much deeper green through the summer, but it's equally elegant in its own way. Prairie dropseed also has two special features: outstanding orange fall color and aromatic flowers (nice if you like the smell of cilantro, I guess).

Native to a wide area of the U.S., prairie dropseed adapts to a wide range of soil conditions. It may self-sow a bit but nowhere near as abundantly as pony tail grass can in warm climates.

Top: Prairie dropseed with Bowman's root (*Gillenia stipulata*), 'Karl Foerster' feather reed grass (*Calamagrostis* x *acutiflora*), and Arkansas bluestar (*Amsonia hubrichtii*) [late October]

Above: Prairie dropseed with Bowman's root, 'Little Henry' sweetspire (*Itea virginica*) and bearsfoot hellebore (*Helleborus foetidus*) [mid-November]

Symphyotrichum

Asters
Asteraceae
Aster Family

It's hard to imagine a fall garden without at least a few asters (*Symphyotrichum*) for height and color.

- Full sun to partial shade
- Average, well-drained soil
- Size varies by species
- Zones 3 or 4-8 or 9

✓ Cheery late-season color
✓ Good winter structure

✗ Some may have disease problems
✗ Tall types may need pruning or staking

Their genus may have changed from the simple *Aster* to the somewhat clumsy-sounding *Symphyotrichum* (among other names), but the North American native asters are still the same reliable performers for late-season borders.

Flower-filled in fall, these asters also offer a good deal of winter beauty, and their fluffy seedheads provide a feast for hungry birds too. Just be aware that the seeds the birds miss are likely to sprout where they land: usually not a big problem if you routinely apply a fresh layer of mulch in spring, but it could lead to some extra weeding if you don't.

Aromatic aster (*Symphyotrichum oblongifolium*) with Joe-Pye weed (*Eutrochium maculatum*) foliage, 'Shenandoah' switch grass (*Panicum virgatum*), and frost aster (*S. pilosum*) [mid-October]

Easy and Pleasing

Aromatic aster (*S. oblongifolium*) is one of my favorite species. The plants form 1- to 2-foot-tall, 2-foot-wide mounds that are dense and bushy without any pruning. They bloom in shades of purple-blue in early to mid-fall and have sturdy stems that don't need staking or pruning. They also tend to hold their form perfectly through the winter months, looking great when dusted with snow.

Top left: Aromatic aster with 'Cassian' fountain grass (*Pennisetum alopecuroides*), 'Skyracer' purple moor grass (*Molinia caerulea* var. *arundinacea*), and 'Sheffield Pink' chrysanthemum [late September]

Top right: Aromatic aster with Briant Rubidor weigela (*Weigela* 'Olympiade') and 'Dropmore Scarlet' honeysuckle (*Lonicera* x *brownii*) [late October]

Left: Aromatic aster with 'Northwind' switch grass (*Panicum virgatum*) [early February]

Lots of Possibilities

Aromatic asters branch out widely from a tight central crown, so there's plenty of room to plant spring bulbs around them for early interest.

In summer, the plants are so tightly mounded that they can double as a boxwood-like edging. Once they bloom, though, you can't mistake them as anything but asters. They combine beautifully with other fall bloomers, with partners that have colorful fall foliage, and with showy seedheads and autumn fruits and berries.

Top left: Aromatic aster with 'Sheffield Pink' chrysanthemum [mid-October]

Top right: Aromatic aster with the fall foliage of Bowman's root (*Gillenia stipulata*) and 'Northwind' switch grass (*Panicum virgatum*) [mid-October]

Right: Aromatic aster with the fruits of 'Flying Dragon' hardy orange (*Poncirus trifoliata*) [mid-October]

Tall for Fall

I love the height and rich pinks and purples of New England asters (*S. novae-angliae*). Left alone, they can easily reach to 6 feet tall, but they may also keel over without sturdy companions. Cut back by half in early summer, they can still reach 4 to 5 feet but produce much neater-looking, self-supporting clumps.

New England asters can be prone to powdery mildew, causing buds to die and lower leaves to drop, especially if the soil dries out. They don't seem to have a big problem in evenly moist soil.

Top left: 'Harrington's Pink' and 'Hella Lacy' New England asters with variegated pokeweed (*Phytolacca americana* 'Silberstein') [mid-September]

Top right: New England asters with heath aster (*S. ericoides*), frost aster (*S. pilosum*), and goldenrod (*Solidago*) [late September]

Left: New England asters with goldenrod (*Solidago*) and Korean feather reed grass (*Calamagrostis brachytricha*) [late September]

Smooth Aster

Native to much of North America, smooth aster (*Symphyotrichum laeve*) looks rather like New England aster, but it has daintier flowers, and it's not prone to powdery mildew. It's also shorter: usually in the 3- to 4-foot range. It thrives in full sun and average, well-drained soil, but it can take a couple hours of shade too. If sprawling is a problem, cut it back by half in early summer.

Top: 'Bluebird' smooth aster (right corner) with purple milkweed (*Asclepias purpurascens*), aromatic aster (*S. oblongifolium*), three-flowered maple (*Acer triflorum*), 'Heavy Metal' switch grass (*Panicum virgatum*), and cut-leaved staghorn sumac (*Rhus typhina* 'Laciniata') [early October]

Right: 'Bluebird' smooth aster with hyssop-leaved boneset (*Eupatorium hyssopifolium*) [late September]

Another Aster

Tatarian aster (*Aster tataricus*), native to parts of Asia, is still a member of the original *Aster* clan, and it blooms in the same lavender-purple that's common in the group. It's a vigorous spreader, to the point of being aggressive, so don't let it go in the loose, rich soil of a regular border; instead, save it for sites with poor, dry soil to slow its spread, or pair it with equally stout companions such as shrubs or tall warm-season grasses.

Tatarian aster is exceptionally late blooming (October into November here), so it's great for adding a touch of fresh color among autumn foliage and seedheads. It can reach 4 to 6 feet tall by bloom time, but the stems are so sturdy that I've never bothered with either pruning or staking.

Top: Tatarian aster with 'The Blues' little bluestem (*Schizachyrium scoparium*) and orange coneflower (*Rudbeckia fulgida* var. *fulgida*) [late October]

Above: Tatarian aster with seven-sons tree (*Heptacodium miconioides*) [mid-November]

Right: Tatarian aster with 'Dallas Blues' switch grass (*Panicum virgatum*), Carolina lupine (*Thermopsis villosa*) seedheads, and 'Cassian' fountain grass (*Pennisetum alopecuroides*) [mid-November]

Symphytum

Comfreys
Boraginaceae
Borage Family

Long valued by herb gardeners, comfreys (*Symphytum*) are also excellent in beds and borders, as long as you choose them carefully.

- Full sun to partial shade
- Average to moist, well-drained soil
- 3-4 feet tall; 3 feet wide
- Zones 4-8

✓ Bold, bright foliage for many months

✗ Variegation may revert to solid green

From an ornamental perspective, the star among the comfreys is 'Axminster Gold', a selection of Russian comfrey (*Symphytum* x *uplandicum*). It's hard to find and kind of expensive to buy, but think of it as an investment. Once it settles in, it happily lives in one spot for many years, slowly expanding into an increasingly spectacular accent.

'Axminster Gold' blooms in late spring to early summer, with pink-to-blue flowers. Unlike many other comfreys, though, this one rarely, if ever, sets seed, so you don't have to worry about it producing unwanted seedlings.

'Axminster Gold' Russian comfrey with 'Queen of Night' tulip, Chocolate Chip ajuga (*Ajuga reptans* 'Valfredda'), lady's mantle (*Alchemilla mollis*), and variegated sweet iris (*Iris pallida* 'Variegata') [early May]

A Charming Companion

The creamy yellow-and-green leaves of 'Axminster Gold' look lovely paired with both bright and pastel pinks, blues, and purples, as well as peachy-colored blooms. And from a textural perspective, spiky or ferny foliage makes an interesting contrast for the broad comfrey leaves.

Top left: 'Axminster Gold' Russian comfrey against 'New Hampshire Purple' bloody cranesbill (*Geranium sanguineum*) and Jacob's ladder (*Polemonium caeruleum*) [late May]

Top right: 'Axminster Gold' Russian comfrey with Guinevere rose (*Rosa* 'Harbadge') [early June]

Left: 'Axminster Gold' Russian comfrey with Chardonnay Pearls slender deutzia (*Deutzia gracilis* 'Duncan'), lady's mantle (*Alchemilla mollis*), and variegated sweet iris (*Iris pallida* 'Variegata') [late May]

91

The Foliage Factor

As soon as the flowers of 'Axminster Gold' drop, cut off the flowering stems at the base and enjoy the broad, hosta-like foliage mound for the rest of the season. Watch for solid-green leaves and dig out those sections right away if they appear.

The foliage may turn brown on the edges if the site is too dry. If it happens repeatedly, move the plant to a shadier spot in the fall or early spring, or add mulch and water during dry spells.

Top: 'Axminster Gold' Russian comfrey with honey bush (*Melianthus major*), 'Dallas Blues' switch grass (*Panicum virgatum*), 'Thompsonii Yellow' flowering maple (*Abutilon pictum*), 'Lime Rickey' heuchera, and 'Silver Falls' ponyfoot (*Dichondra argentea*) [mid-July]

Right: 'Axminster Gold' Russian comfrey with 'Cherry Brandy' Gloriosa daisy (*Rudbeckia hirta*) [late July]

Another Symphytum

Yellow or dwarf comfrey (*Symphytum grandiflorum*) is as subtle as 'Axminster Gold' is spectacular, but it has a quiet charm of its own, with over a month of reddish buds that open to cream-colored bells on 1-foot-tall stems in late spring. After bloom, it's just deep green leaves for the rest of the year, with dense crowns that spread to form solid carpets.

When I say "spread," I mean serious creeping: a trait that makes yellow comfrey a scary choice for most borders but an excellent choice as a ground cover. It thrives in rich, moist soil in partial shade but can adapt to anything from full sun to shade. It's one of my go-to plants for dry shade — especially for filling space under deciduous shrubs. Best of all, deer don't seem to like the leaves. Yellow comfrey is hardy in Zones 3 or 4 to 9.

Top: Yellow comfrey (*Symphytum grandiflorum*) against 'Espresso' wild geranium (*Geranium maculatum*) [late April]

Above: Yellow comfrey with 'Espresso' wild geranium, 'Sunshine' red-twig dogwood (*Cornus sericea* subsp. *occidentalis*), and variegated sweet iris (*Iris pallida* 'Variegata') [mid-May]

Vernonia

Ironweeds
Asteraceae
Aster Family

Ironweeds (*Vernonia*) are tall and tough: ideal for adding height and color to late-season borders.

- Full sun to light shade
- Average to moist soil
- 6-8 feet tall; 1-3 feet wide
- Zones 5-9

✓ Bright flowers for fall
✓ Sturdy stems rarely need staking

✗ Can self-sow prolifically
✗ Rust fungus can discolor leaves

Ironweeds (*Vernonia*) can bloom when very young, at just 2 or 3 feet tall, but over time, they typically top out at 6 feet or more. They're best suited for the back of a border, but if you really want to keep them shorter, experiment with cutting them back by half (or a third, or two-thirds) in early to midsummer.

My only disappointment with the ironweeds — especially New York ironweed (*V. noveboracensis*) — is their susceptibility to fungal rust. The leaf damage is unattractive but usually doesn't appear until late summer or fall, and it doesn't seem to interfere with the bloom or the overall vigor of the plants.

Tall ironweed (*Vernonia gigantea*) with orange coneflower (*Rudbeckia fulgida* var. *fulgida*), 'Karl Foerster' feather reed grass (*Calamagrostis* x *acutiflora*), 'Karley Rose' Oriental fountain grass (*Pennisetum orientale*), golden elderberry (*Sambucus nigra* 'Aurea'), 'Temptation' Culver's root (*Veronicastrum virginicum*), 'Rotstrahlbusch' switch grass (*Panicum virgatum*), Joe-Pye weed (*Eutrochium maculatum*), and 'Fireworks' goldenrod (*Solidago rugosa*) [mid-August]

High Style

Ironweeds' rich violet-purple combines cheerily with other tall late-bloomers for early fall color in sunny borders. Pair them with typical autumn perennials such as asters (*Symphyotrichum*) and grasses, or mix them up with long-blooming annuals and colorful foliage for unexpected effects.

Top left: Tall ironweed (*Vernonia gigantea*) with 'Coppelia' sneezeweed (*Helenium*), 'Strawberry Fields' globe amaranth (*Gomphrena haageana*), 'Red Spider' zinnia (*Zinnia tenuifolia*), 'Sweet Caroline Yellow Green' sweet potato vine (*Ipomoea batatas*), and 'Bishop of Llandaff' dahlia [late August]

Top right: New York ironweed (*V. noveboracensis*) with golden catalpa (*Catalpa bignonioides* 'Aurea'), 'Aztec Orange' zinnia (*Zinnia elegans*), and orange coneflower (*Rudbeckia fulgida* var. *fulgida*) [late August]

Left: Ironweed with variegated pokeweed (*Phytolacca americana* 'Silberstein') [mid-September]

Heads above the Rest

Even better than the ironweeds' blooms are their fluffy, ball-like seedheads. They show off particularly well against dark backgrounds, but they're also exquisite when backlit by the rising or setting sun.

In late fall, many of the seeds will drop and produce seedlings the following spring, which can lead to a lot of weeding. As a compromise, I leave the seedheads on for most of October, then cut them off as soon as I see the seeds starting to fall.

Top left: Ironweed seedheads with 'Hella Lacy' New England aster (*Symphyotrichum novae-angliae*) and purple fountain grass (*Pennisetum setaceum* 'Rubrum') [early October]

Top right: Ironweed seedheads against New England aster [mid-October]

Left: Ironweed seedheads with Diabolo ninebark (*Physocarpus opulifolius* 'Monlo') [late October]

Another Vernonia

And now for something completely different from the typical towering species: narrow-leaved ironweed (*Vernonia lettermannii*). This one looks far more like an Arkansas bluestar (*Amsonia hubrichtii*) — particularly in the selection 'Iron Butterfly' — with very slender, deep green leaves in dense mounds about 2 feet tall and wide. Unlike the spring-blooming bluestar, though, narrow-leaved ironweed flowers in early fall, in the usual ironweed purple, followed by the usual fluffy seedheads later in the season.

Narrow-leaved ironweed offers a fun alternative to the usual mums and asters for fall flowers at the front of a border.

Top: Narrow-leaved ironweed (*Vernonia lettermannii*) [mid-September]

Above: 'Iron Butterfly' narrow-leaved ironweed with orange coneflower (*Rudbeckia fulgida* var. *fulgida*) [mid-September]

Right: 'Iron Butterfly' narrow-leaved ironweed seedheads with the fall foliage of golden lace (*Patrinia scabiosifolia*) [mid-November]

Veronicastrum

Culver's Roots

Scrophulariaceae
Figwort Family

Wispy white spikes make Culver's root (*Veronicastrum virginicum*) a dramatic choice for midsummer color and showy autumn seedheads.

- Full sun to partial shade
- Average to moist soil
- 4-7 feet tall; 1-2 feet wide
- Zones 3-8

✓ Spiky flower- and seedheads offer interesting contrast to common flower forms

✗ May need support in windy sites

Native to much of the eastern half of North America, Culver's root (*Veronicastrum virginicum*) is a sadly overlooked summer perennial. Like many of my other favorites, it takes several years to really settle in, but it's worth the wait, because it just keeps getting better and rarely needs any fussing.

Pest insects seldom bother the foliage of Culver's root, but beneficial insects love the densely packed spikes of pollen- and nectar-rich blooms. Butterflies flock to them too, and some birds feed on the seeds, so Culver's root is a great choice if you're looking to attract wildlife to your garden.

Culver's root with purple coneflower (*Echinacea purpurea*) and cut-leaved staghorn sumac (*Rhus typhina* 'Laciniata') [early July]

To Cut or Not

Culver's root looks fantastic in masses in large borders, paired with sturdy companions that the slender stems can lean on and mingle with. In smaller spaces, you could stake the clumps, or else try cutting them back by half in late May; this produces much denser and somewhat shorter clumps and delays bloom by a few weeks too. Sheared clumps lose the willowy charm of the taller plants, though.

Top: Culver's root — sheared clump on left and unsheared clump on right — with 'Australia' canna and 'Plum Crazy' rose mallow (*Hibiscus*) [late July]

Left: Culver's root with purple coneflower (*Echinacea purpurea*), false indigo (*Baptisia australis*), and little bluestem (*Schizachyrium scoparium*) [early July]

Striking Spikes

Here in Pennsylvania, Culver's root blooms through July; it can be a month earlier or later in southern or northern areas. After that, you get to enjoy the dried spires through fall and much of the winter, too. They show up beautifully against showy fall foliage as well as winter-bleached grasses, and they make a dramatic contrast to rounded seedheads, such as those of bee balms (*Monarda*) and coneflowers (*Echinacea* and *Rudbeckia*).

Top left: Culver's root seedheads with frost aster (*Symphyotrichum pilosum*) and orange coneflower (*Rudbeckia fulgida* var. *fulgida*) against 'Northwind' switch grass (*Panicum virgatum*) [mid-October]

Top right: Culver's root seedheads against 'Rotstrahlbusch' switch grass [early December]

Right: Culver's root seedheads with 'Jacob Cline' bee balm (*Monarda*) [mid-December]

Culver's Roots in Other Colors

Culver's root (*Veronicastrum virginicum*) is commonly thought of as a white flower, but there's actually a fair bit of color variation, giving rise to a growing number of named selections. With so many daisy-form flowers in the summer garden, it's great to have the extra color options among these striking spikes.

'Temptation' is one of the purply ones, with a rather loose collection of spikes atop each of the 4- to 5-foot-tall stems. Its growth habit is also rather loose, which looks charming in informal borders.

'Erica' has a much more upright growth habit even without pruning or staking, and it reaches just 3 to 4 feet tall. The spring foliage is heavily blushed with purple-red, eventually turning deep green, and the dense flower spikes are pale pink.

Top: 'Temptation' Culver's root with 'Rotstrahlbusch' switch grass (*Panicum virgatum*), purple coneflower (*Echinacea purpurea*) and golden elderberry (*Sambucus nigra* 'Aurea') [mid-July]

Above: 'Erica' Culver's root with campion (*Silene dioica*) and 'Queen of Night' tulip [early May]

Right: 'Erica' Culver's Root with summer phlox (*Phlox paniculata*) [mid-July]

'Axminster Gold' Russian comfrey (*Symphytum* x *uplandicum*) with Guinevere rose (*Rosa* 'Harbadge') [late May]

Page numbers in **bold** indicate main entries
Page numbers in *italics* indicate photographs

Index

Ageratina (snakeroots): 35
   A. altissima (snakeroot): 35
      A. altissima 'Prairie Jewel': 35
   A. aromatica 'Jocius' Variegate' (lesser snakeroot): 35; *35, 65*
Alchemilla mollis (lady's mantle): *90, 91*
Allium (alliums, ornamental onions): 45
   A. sphaerocephalon (drumstick chives): *9*
   A. 'White Giant': *45*
Alumroots. See *Heuchera*
Amsonia (bluestars): **8-13**
   A. 'Blue Ice': 13; *13*
   A. hubrichtii (Arkansas bluestar): 8-12, 56; *8, 9, 18, 30, 31, 60, 61, 67, 83*
Anthemis 'Susanna Mitchell': *15*
Arkansas bluestar. See *Amsonia hubrichtii*
Artemisia (artemisia)
   A. abrotanum (southernwood): *49*
   A. 'Powis Castle': *45, 46*
Asclepias purpurascens (purple milkweed): *51, 88*
Aster, *Aster* (asters) (See also *Symphyotrichum*)
   aromatic. See *Symphyotrichum oblongifolium*
   A. tataricus (Tatarian aster): 89; *6-7, 89*
   frost. See *Symphyotrichum pilosum*
   heath. See *Symphyotrichum ericoides*
   New England. See *Symphyotrichum novae-angliae*
   smooth. See *Symphyotrichum laeve*
   Tatarian. See *Aster tataricus*
Autumn crocus. See *Colchicum*

Baptisia (false indigos): **14-19**
   B. alba (white false indigo): 19; *19, 29*
   B. australis (blue false indigo): 19; *19, 99*
   B. 'Carolina Moonlight': 17; *17*
   B. 'Purple Smoke': 18; *9, 18*
   B. sphaerocarpa 'Screamin' Yellow' (yellow false indigo): 14-17; *14, 15, 16, 82*
   B. 'Twilite' [Twilite Prairieblues]: 18; *18*
Bee balm. See *Monarda* 'Jacob Cline'
Betony, wood. See *Stachys officinalis*
Blood grass. See *Imperata cylindrica* 'Rubra'
Bluebeard. See *Caryopteris incana*
Blue flax. See *Linum perenne*
Blue mist shrub. See *Caryopteris* x *clandonensis*

Bluestars. See *Amsonia*
Bluestem, little. See *Schizachyrium scoparium*
Bonesets. See *Eupatorium*
Bowman's root. See *Gillenia stipulata*
Brazilian vervain. See *Verbena bonariensis*
Burnets. See *Sanguisorba*
Bush honeysuckle, southern. See *Diervilla sessilifolia*

Calamagrostis (feather reed grasses): **20-23**
   C. x *acutiflora* 'Karl Foerster' (feather reed grass): 20-22; *1, 20, 21, 31, 32, 53, 63, 78, 83, 94*
   C. brachytricha (Korean feather reed grass): 23; *23, 87*
Carex (sedges)
   C. muskingumensis 'Oehme' (palm sedge): *38*
   C. plantaginea (plantain-leaved sedge): *23*
Carolina lupine. See *Thermopsis villosa*
Caryopteris (caryopteris)
   C. x *clandonensis* 'Worcester Gold' (blue mist shrub): *24*
   C. incana (bluebeard)
      C. incana 'Jason' [Sunshine Blue]: *45*
      C. incana 'Snow Fairy': *78*
Catmint. See *Nepeta* 'Walker's Low'
Chasmanthium latifolium (northern sea oats): *50, 71*
Chrysanthemum (chrysanthemums)
   orange: *66*
   'Sheffield Pink': *46, 85, 86*
Colchicum (autumn crocuses)
   C. autumnale: *76*
   C. 'Waterlily': *51*
Comfreys. See *Symphytum*
Coneflowers. See *Echinacea* and *Rudbeckia*
Cornus (dogwoods)
   C. sericea 'Cardinal' (red-twig dogwood): *82*
   C. sericea 'Silver and Gold' (yellow-twig dogwood): *81*
   C. sericea subsp. *occidentalis* 'Sunshine' (red-twig dogwood): *93*
Crambe maritima (sea kale): *78*
Culver's roots. See *Veronicastrum*

Diervilla sessilifolia (southern bush honeysuckle): *47*
Dogwoods. See *Cornus*
Dropseed, prairie. See *Sporobolus heterolepis*

Echinacea (purple coneflowers): **24-29**
   E. 'Evan Saul' [Sundown]: 29; *29*
   E. 'Matthew Saul' [Harvest Moon]: *82*
   E. pallida (pale purple coneflower): 29; *29*
   E. purpurea (purple coneflower): 24-28; *1, 21, 24, 25, 26, 27, 28, 29, 37, 47, 53, 60, 61, 62, 99, 101*
Elderberries. See *Sambucus*
Eryngium (sea holly): *79*
Eucomis comosa 'Oakhurst' (pineapple lily): *77*
Eupatoriadelphus. See *Eutrochium*
Eupatorium (bonesets): 35 (See also *Eutrochium*)
   E. hyssopifolium (hyssop-leaved boneset): 35; *35, 88*
Eutrochium (Joe-Pye weeds): **30-35**
   E. dubium 'Little Joe' (Joe-Pye weed): 33; *33, 74*
   E. fistulosum (Joe-Pye weed): 30
   E. maculatum (Joe-Pye weed): 30-32, 34; *1, 13, 20, 25, 30, 31, 32, 34, 35, 50, 55, 61, 78, 84, 94*
     E. maculatum 'Carin': 32; *11, 12, 31, 38*
     E. maculatum 'Gateway': 32; *32, 34*
   E. purpureum (Joe-Pye weed): 30

Fallopia baldschuanica 'Lemon Lace' (silver fleece vine): *21, 30, 50*
False indigos. See *Baptisia*
Feather grass, Mexican. See *Stipa tenuissima*
Feather reed grasses. See *Calamagrostis*
Fleeceflowers. See *Persicaria*
Fountain grasses. See *Pennisetum*
Frost grass. See *Spodiopogon sibiricus*

Geranium (hardy geraniums)
   G. maculatum 'Espresso' (wild geranium): *93*
   G. sanguineum 'New Hampshire Purple' (bloody cranesbill): *91*
Germander, sticky. See *Teucrium viscidum* 'Lemon and Lime'
Ghost bramble. See *Rubus thibetanus* 'Silver Fern'
Gillenia stipulata (Bowman's root): *27, 52, 83, 86*
Gloriosa daisy. See *Rudbeckia hirta* 'Cherry Brandy'
Golden elderberry. See *Sambucus nigra* 'Aurea'
Golden lace. See *Patrinia scabiosifolia*
Goldenrods. See *Solidago*
Grasses.
   bitter switch grass. See *Panicum amarum* 'Dewey Blue'
   blood grass, Japanese. See *Imperata cylindrica* 'Rubra'
   bluestem, little. See *Schizachyrium scoparium*
   dropseed, prairie. See *Sporobolus heterolepis*
   feather grass, Mexican. See *Stipa tenuissima*

Grasses (continued)
   feather reed grasses. See *Calamagrostis*
   fountain grasses. See *Pennisetum*
   frost grass. See *Spodiopogon sibiricus*
   Indian grass. See *Sorghastrum nutans*
   Japanese blood grass. See *Imperata cylindrica* 'Rubra'
   Korean feather reed grass. See *Calamagrostis brachytricha*
   little bluestem. See *Schizachyrium scoparium*
   Mexican feather grass. See *Stipa tenuissima*
   miscanthus. See *Miscanthus sinensis* 'Morning Light'
   moor grasses. See *Molinia*
   muhly grass, pink. See *Muhlenbergia capillaris*
   northern sea oats. See *Chasmanthium latifolium*
   Oriental fountain grass. See *Pennisetum orientale* 'Karley Rose'
   pink muhly grass. See *Muhlenbergia capillaris*
   pony tail grasses. See *Stipa*
   prairie dropseed. See *Sporobolus heterolepis*
   purple moor grass. See *Molinia caerulea* subsp. *arundinacea*
   sedges. See *Carex*
   switch grasses. See *Panicum*

Hardy orange. See *Poncirus trifoliata* 'Flying Dragon'
Helenium 'Coppelia' (sneezeweed): *72, 73, 95*
Helianthus (sunflowers): **36-39**
   H. 'Lemon Queen' (perennial sunflower): 36-38; *26, 36, 37, 38, 62, 73*
   H. salicifolius 'Low Down' (willow-leaved sunflower): 39; *39*
Heliopsis helianthoides 'Loraine Sunshine': *78*
Heuchera (heucheras, alumroots): **40-43**
   H. 'Caramel': 41; *40, 41, 43*
   H. 'Creme Brulee': 41
   H. 'Obsidian': 42; *42*
   H. 'Peach Flambe': 41; *41*
   H. 'Southern Comfort': 41
   H. 'Stormy Seas': *45*
   H. villosa (hairy alumroot): 41
     H. villosa 'Autumn Bride': 42; *42*
Hylotelephium telephium 'Gooseberry Fool': *32*

Imperata cylindrica 'Rubra' (Japanese blood grass): *11, 25, 67, 77*
Indian grass. See *Sorghastrum nutans*
Iris pallida 'Variegata' (variegated sweet iris): *90, 91, 93*
Ironweeds. See *Vernonia*

Japanese blood grass. See *Imperata cylindrica* 'Rubra'
Japanese burnet. See *Sanguisorba tenuifolia*
Japanese emperor oak. See *Quercus dentata*
Joe-Pye weeds. See *Eutrochium*

Korean feather reed grass. See *Calamagrostis brachytricha*

Lady's mantle. See *Alchemilla mollis*
Lamb's ears. See *Stachys*
Lemon balm. See *Melissa officinalis* 'All Gold'
Leucanthemum 'Becky' (Shasta daisy): *49*
Lilium 'Black Beauty' (Orienpet lily): *31*
Linum perenne (blue flax): *75*
Little bluestem. See *Schizachyrium scoparium*
Lupine, Carolina. See *Thermopsis villosa*

Marguerite. See *Anthemis* 'Susanna Mitchell'
Melissa officinalis 'All Gold': *41*
Mexican feather grass. See *Stipa tenuissima*
Milkweed, purple. See *Asclepias purpurascens*
Miscanthus sinensis 'Morning Light' (miscanthus): *33, 39, 71*
Molinia (moor grasses): **44-47**
  M. caerulea subsp. *arundinacea* (purple moor grass): 44-46
    M. caerulea subsp. *arundinacea* 'Bergfreund': *45, 46*
    M. caerulea subsp. *arundinacea* 'Skyracer': *27, 44, 46, 59, 60, 85*
  M. caerulea 'Variegata' (variegated moor grass): *13*
Monarda 'Jacob Cline': *100*
Moor grasses. See *Molinia*
Muhlenbergia capillaris (pink muhly grass): *11, 22*
Muhly grass. See *Muhlenbergia capillaris*

Nassella tenuissima. See *Stipa tenuissima*
Nepeta 'Walker's Low' (catmint): *15*
Ninebark. See *Physocarpus opulifolius*
Northern sea oats. See *Chasmanthium latifolium*

Oak, Japanese emperor. See *Quercus dentata*
Onions, ornamental. See *Allium*
Orange coneflowers. See *Rudbeckia*
Ornamental onions. See *Allium*
Oxeye. See *Heliopsis helianthoides* 'Loraine Sunshine'

Panicum (switch grasses): **48-53**
  P. amarum 'Dewey Blue' (bitter switch grass): 53; *33, 53, 107*
  P. virgatum (switch grass): 48
    P. virgatum 'Cloud Nine': *26, 61, 62*
    P. virgatum 'Dallas Blues': *48, 49, 70, 89, 92*
    P. virgatum 'Heavy Metal': 51; *51, 88*
    P. virgatum 'Northwind': 52; *27, 36, 52, 85, 86, 100*
    P. virgatum 'Rotstrahlbusch': *25, 69, 94, 100, 101*
    P. virgatum 'Shenandoah': 50; *50, 84*
Patrinia (patrinias): **54-57**
  P. scabiosifolia (golden lace): 54-57; *1, 6, 53, 54, 55, 56, 57, 59, 97*
Pennisetum (fountain grasses): **58-61**
  P. alopecuroides (fountain grass): 58-59; *28, 55, 57, 58, 59, 69*
    P. alopecuroides 'Cassian': 60; *4-5, 27, 33, 47, 52, 59, 60, 70, 85, 89*
  P. orientalis 'Karley Rose' (Oriental fountain grass): 61; *61, 94*
Persicaria (fleeceflowers): **62-67**
  P. affine 'Dimity' (dwarf or Himalayan fleeceflower): 67; *11*
  P. amplexicaulis (mountain fleeceflower): 66
    P. amplexicaulis 'Taurus': *66*
  P. 'Crimson Beauty': 65; *65*
  P. polymorpha (giant fleeceflower): 63-64; *9, 13, 14, 50, 62, 63, 64, 74*
Physocarpus opulifolius (ninebark)
  P. opulifolius 'Center Glow': *63*
  P. opulifolius 'Monlo' [Diabolo]: *23, 25, 29, 96*
Phytolacca americana 'Silberstein' (variegated pokeweed): *87, 95*
Pineapple lily. See *Eucomis comosa* 'Oakhurst'
Pink muhly grass. See *Muhlenbergia capillaris*
Pokeweed, variegated. See *Phytolacca americana* 'Silberstein'
Poncirus trifoliata 'Flying Dragon' (hardy orange): *86*
Pony tail grasses. See *Stipa*
Porteranthus. See *Gillenia stipulata*
Prairie dropseed. See *Sporobolus heterolepis*
Purple coneflowers. See *Echinacea*
Purple moor grass. See *Molinia caerulea* subsp. *arundinacea*

Quercus dentata (Japanese emperor oak): *49, 64, 70*

Rhus typhina (staghorn sumac)
  R. typhina 'Bailtiger' [Tiger Eyes]: *50*
  R. typhina 'Laciniata' (cut-leaved staghorn sumac): *51, 88, 98*

Rosa (roses)
   R. 'Frau Dagmar Hastrup': *8, 61*
   R. *glauca* (red-leaved rose): *31*
   R. 'Harbadge' [Guinevere]: *91, 102*
   R. 'Radrazz' [Knock Out]: *26, 63*
Rubus thibetanus 'Silver Fern' (ghost bramble): *9*
Rudbeckia (orange coneflowers): **68-71**
   R. *fulgida* var. *fulgida* (orange coneflower): 68-70; *1, 26, 32, 36, 37, 47, 48, 49, 52, 53, 55, 57, 60, 68, 69, 70, 89, 94, 95, 97, 100*
   R. *hirta* 'Cherry Brandy' (Gloriosa daisy): *92*
   R. *maxima* (giant coneflower): 71; *30, 52, 71*

Salix alba var. *sericea* (silver willow): *13, 14, 55, 58, 63, 65*
Salvia 'Caradonna': *14, 15, 78*
Sambucus (elderberries)
   S. *nigra* 'Aurea' (golden elderberry): *25, 26, 73, 94, 101*
   S. *racemosa* 'Sutherland Gold': *21, 45*
Sanguisorba (burnets): **72-75**
   S. *menziesii* 'Dali Marble': 75; *75*
   S. *officinalis* 'Tanna': 75; *75*
   S. *tenuifolia* (Japanese burnet): 72
     S. *tenuifolia* 'Alba' (white Japanese burnet): 74; *74*
     S. *tenuifolia* 'Purpurea' (purple Japanese burnet): 72-73; *72, 73*
Schizachyrium scoparium (little bluestem): *35, 62, 70, 99*
   S. *scoparium* 'Blaze': *20, 22*
   S. *scoparium* 'The Blues': *1, 53, 89, 107*
Sea kale. See *Crambe maritima*
Sedum (sedums) (See also *Hylotelephium telephium* 'Gooseberry Fool')
   S. 'Purple Emperor': *31, 77*
   S. *rupestre* 'Angelina': *8, 12, 42, 46*
Shasta daisy. See *Leucanthemum* 'Becky'
Silver fleece vine. See *Fallopia baldschuanica* 'Lemon Lace'
Silver willow. See *Salix alba* var. *sericea*
Snakeroots. See *Ageratina*
Sneezeweed. See *Helenium* 'Coppelia'
Solidago (goldenrods): *35, 66, 87*
   S. *rugosa* 'Fireworks': 57; *27, 57, 58, 59, 94*
Sorghastrum nutans (Indian grass): *33, 37*
Southern bush honeysuckle. See *Diervilla sessilifolia*
Spodiopogon sibiricus (frost grass): 47; *47, 59, 60*
Sporobolus heterolepis (prairie dropseed): 58, 83; *83*
Stachys (lamb's ears): **76-79**
   S. *byzantina* (lamb's ears): 76, 78; *77, 78*
     S. *byzantina* 'Big Ears' ('Helene von Stein'): 76-77; *20, 22, 68, 76, 77, 78*

Stachys (continued)
   S. *officinalis* (wood betony): 79; *79*
     S. *officinalis* 'Alba': 79; *79*
Stipa (pony tail grasses): **80-83**
   S. *tenuissima* (pony tail grass, Mexican feather grass): 80-82; *14, 41, 80, 81, 82*
Sumac, staghorn. See *Rhus typhina*
Sunflowers. See *Helianthus*
Switch grasses. See *Panicum*
Symphyotrichum (asters): **84-89**
   S. *ericoides* (heath aster): *87*
   S. *laeve* (smooth aster): 88
     S. *laeve* 'Bluebird': *35, 51, 69, 88*
   S. *novae-angliae* (New England aster): 87; *56, 96*
     S. *novae-angliae* 'Alma Potschke': *59*
     S. *novae-angliae* 'Harrington's Pink': *37, 87*
     S. *novae-angliae* 'Hella Lacy': *87, 96*
   S. *oblongifolium* (aromatic aster): 85-86; *4-5, 27, 28, 44, 46, 48, 50, 51, 52, 56, 58, 59, 74, 75, 81, 84, 85, 88*
   S. *pilosum* (frost aster): *50, 84, 100*
Symphytum (comfreys): **90-93**
   S. *grandiflorum* (yellow comfrey, dwarf comfrey): 93; *93*
   S. x *uplandicum* 'Axminster Gold' (Russian comfrey): 90-92; *90, 91, 92, 102*

Tanacetum vulgare 'Isla Gold' (tansy): *66*
Tansy. See *Tanacetum vulgare* 'Isla Gold'
Teucrium viscidum 'Lemon and Lime' (sticky germander): *42*
Thermopsis villosa (Carolina lupine): *89*
Tulip 'Queen of Night': *90, 101*

Verbena bonariensis (Brazilian vervain): *58, 59, 81*
Vernonia (ironweeds): **94-97**; *2-3, 32, 37, 38, 55, 57*
   V. *gigantea* (tall ironweed): *26, 61, 73, 94, 95*
   V. *lettermannii* (narrow-leaved ironweed): 97; *97*
     V. *lettermannii* 'Iron Butterfly': 97; *97*
   V. *noveboracensis* (New York ironweed): *94*
Veronicastrum (Culver's roots): **98-101**
   V. *virginicum*: 98-101; *98, 99, 100*
   V. *virginicum* 'Erica': 101; *101*
   V. *virginicum* 'Temptation': 101; *94, 101, 107*

Weigela (weigelas)
   W. *florida* 'Bramwell' [Fine Wine]: *25*
   W. 'Olympiade' [Briant Rubidor]: *38, 85*
Willow, silver. See *Salix alba* var. *sericea*
Wood betony. See *Stachys officinalis*

'Temptation' Culver's root (*Veronicastrum virginicum*) with 'The Blues' little bluestem (*Schizachyrium scoparium*) and 'Dewey Blue' bitter switch grass (*Panicum amarum*) [late September]

About the Author

Nancy J. Ondra lives in Bucks County, Pennsylvania (mid-Zone 6 to lower Zone 7, depending on the hardiness zone map you use). Nan's garden, which she calls Hayefield, includes four acres in full sun: about two acres of managed meadow; one acre of pasture for her alpaca companions, Daniel and Duncan; and one acre of intensively planted borders and open shrubbery areas.

Nan is the author or co-author of over a dozen gardening books, among them:

- *The Perennial Care Manual*
- *Foliage: Astonishing Color and Texture beyond Flowers*
- *Fallscaping*
- *The Perennial Gardener's Design Primer*
- *Taylor's Guide to Roses*
- *Grasses: Versatile Partners for Uncommon Garden Design*

She also writes about her favorite plants, combinations, and gardening projects at her blog, Hayefield (*www.hayefield.com*).

Made in the USA
Lexington, KY
24 April 2018